30 Ways To Make Money...
In Writing

by

Jennie Hawthorne

Series Editor:
Luke Johnson

Rushmere Wynne
England

First published 1989
This edition 1996

© Jennie Hawthorne

All rights reserved. No part of this publication may be reproduced, stored in a retrieval system, or transmitted, in any form or by any means, electronic, mechanical, photocopying, recording or otherwise, without the prior permission of the publishers.

The right of Jennie Hawthorne to be identified as the author of this work has been asserted by her in accordance with the Copyright, Designs and Patents Act 1988.

British Library Cataloguing in Publication Data. A catalogue record for this book is available from the British Library.

ISBN 0 948035 26 9

Designed and typeset by:
MacWing

Photography by:
Malcolm Burden

Published by:
Rushmere Wynne Group Plc
4-5 Harmill, Grovebury Road,
Leighton Buzzard, Bedfordshire LU7 8FF
Tel: 01525 853726
Fax: 01525 852037

Printed by:
H. S. Printers
4-5 Harmill, Grovebury Road,
Leighton Buzzard, Bedfordshire LU7 8FF

30 Ways To Make Money...
In Writing

by

Jennie Hawthorne

Contents

Acknowledgements	7
Introduction	9
Why Writing? The Ten Golden Rules Of The Writing Business	11
The Feature Article	17
The Religious Press	21
Business Communication	25
Biography	29
Writing For Children	33
Competitions And Awards	37
Letters	43
The Free Press	47
The Education Market	51
Text Books	57
Confessions	61
The Trade Press	65
Ghost Writing	69
Poetry	73
How-To-Do-It	79
Develop A Specialism	83
Self Help	87
Writing Speeches	91
The Story Of Your Life	95
Humour	101
Writing A Novel	107
The Short Story	111
Radio Scripts	115
Radio Plays	119

	Live Theatre	123
	Song Writing	127
	Jingles	133
	Films	137
	Teaching	141
	TV (With Specimen Script)	145
Appendix:	Further Reading	155

Acknowledgements

For any merit this book may have, thanks are due to my parents and Sister Hedwig, late headmistress of St. Anne's School, Whitechapel E1; to Notre Dame School, Southwark SE1, and Plater College, Oxford, all of whom tried, not quite in vain, to make a silk purse out of a sow's ear; to editors and publishers perspicacious —or reckless – enough to take and even pay for my work; to my family: Francine and Kathy for their narrative powers; Michael for his computer wizardry; Jennifer for her imagination; John for his unfailing optimism; Stephanie, editor of Pensions World and contributor to many magazines, for her expert financial and technical guidance; Jeremy for his firm faith; sister-in-law Bella for her gift of friendship; daughters-in-law, Breda and Jan for their Irish and Scottish beauty (and accents); to my lovely grandchildren for all the virtues that grandchildren possess, and finally to husband Frank, for showing me his electronic transmission. . . and other skills.

Acknowledgements are hereby made to Guardian Assurance for permission to use the TV script featuring their insurance scheme, FREEDOM.

Introduction

I hope this book sheds a little light on the magic of words and helps you to use them with care. Seeing the excellence that others have achieved with their pen might inspire you to do likewise.

Medieval craftsmen laboured with love on cathedral roof-top carvings because their work, invisible to the human eye, could be seen by God. Your work, too, is going out to readers and viewers equally invisible to you.

Touch them with your style, your vision, your knowledge, your wit, your humour, your skill. You may not share the faith of Fontaine, but you will understand him when he writes, "There is this consolation in the work that one undertakes for God, that He asks of us the work itself, not its success."

Making money from writing, like making money from other skills, is only one measure, often imperfect, of its worth. A child does not pay for the care received while growing up, yet that job may be of more benefit to individuals and society than the highly paid work of countless others.

Believe in yourself and your product. Distinguish between justice, which is owed to you as a labourer worthy of your hire, and charity, which you owe to others as part of humankind. Be prepared to argue for a just wage, if not for yourself, for any who lack your strength. When, by luck or judgement, you make your pile, treat it like muck 'not good except it be spread.' You will then be doubly blessed, for those who are unfortunate enough not to have read your work will gain from your *largesse*.

Now stop reading about writing, and take up your pen.

Why Writing?
The Ten Golden Rules Of The Writing Business

This book tells you how to make money from writing. There are other reasons for putting pen to paper, or hands on word processors. Some of them are far more worthy, some more compelling. You may want to plead a cause, remedy an injustice, shine in an exam, write a letter to your beloved. If so, you will have to rely not on the contents of this book, but on your style or your passion, for the following pages deal only with the possibility of earning an income of sorts from, initially, the written word.

That income may be small, large, infrequent, or a regular sum which keeps away the howling of wolves from your door. But in learning how to interest an editor sufficiently to buy your work, you also learn how to interest, inform or entertain others. And if you are still not convinced of the possibilities and advantages in writing for money, here are ten of them to think about:

30 Ways To Make Money – **IN WRITING**

1 Writing can be done anywhere you please: while travelling in plane or train, at home or abroad. Unless you are writing about a luxury hotel or some specific location, you gain no advantage by being in the actual place. Sean O'Casey wrote his first novel on a park bench. O. Henry (William Sydney Porter) was in prison when he wrote his first story. Unless facts and figures are wanted, you can let your imagination run riot, wherever you are. You have only one job and one aim: to produce readable copy that will sell.

2 Writing for profit need not take up all your energy and time. You can work for only part of the day. . . or night. The amount of time you give to your writing depends largely on yourself. You can start in a small way, for example, by writing to a magazine or paper, a letter which could win a prize for the best letter contributed that week. You can enter a competition for the best line on some wonderful new product or plot out a year's output for a biography or other lengthy work.

3 Age does not matter. You could be the youngest person that ever wrote for money or the oldest. Howard Spring used to touch his finished works on the upturned trunk of a Copenhagen stoneware elephant before sending them off for publication. His wife, Marion Howard Spring, says in her introduction to his *Eleven Stories and a Beginning* (published by Collins): "When I began to write at the age of seventy-four, I followed suit, and *Memories and Gardens,* all paid homage to the elephant before going on their journey. If I live to finish this book – I am now in my eighty-first year – I shall once more ask the elephant to bless my work." Mary Ogilvie was 93 when she wrote *A Scottish Childhood– and What Happened After,* and Mary Wesley 70 when she turned out her first book in 1986.

4 Disability need not deter you. Strength and good health are not required. Many severely disabled people have written marvellously helpful and inspiring books, even when severely handicapped. Christy Brown, one of 19 children, was paralysed in all but his left foot which he used to write his best seller, *My Left Foot.* George Thomas, while bedridden, wrote three books in five years by using a weight attached to his hand. Edith Bone was denied writing materials when confined to an Hungarian prison. She pulled out strands of her hair and with rolled up breadcrumbs made an abacus to work out mathematical problems to retain her sanity. She wrote an autobiography when she finally emerged.

5 Unless you are writing an academic treatise, which usually brings you in little but status (there are exceptions), you do not have to possess any qualifications. All you need is to be able to interest an audience. And you can even choose your own audience. Your writing can be as simple or as complex, as specialised or as general as you wish. You can go for short or long pieces, a simple letter or slogan, a complex article or book. As long as you keep your main aim in view of selling whatever you write, the world is your oyster.

6 Your background is unimportant. Your skin colour can be black, white, red, yellow. You can be of any race or religion: there are no barriers in the writing world. Indeed, the fact that you feel or are 'different' in some way from the people around you is a positive advantage. You are able to write from a unique point of view. You have the virtue of originality. Chinua Achebe's *Man of the People* and *Things Fall Apart* tell us far more of Nigeria than many tomes, and in my opinion are superior to his Booker Prize nomination many years later.

Ruth Prawer Jhabvalla, Polish by birth, married to an Indian architect, made the characters taken from the country of her adoption come alive even before the Merchant Ivory team put them on film. Dorothy Scannell, one of nine children, wrote about her East End background with charming simplicity in her book, *Mother Knows Best.* You do not need a pretty face, handsome profile or to be the most popular person on the campus. These attractions may help you initially to get an introduction to some powerful publisher, but unless you marry him or turn out copy that people want to read, you won't last long. Writing is like entertainment or sport: ask yourself not what you feel or look like, but can you perform?

7 There are no start up costs. You do not have to provide equipment or factory space, to hunt around for funds for yourself or others. You do not have to go, cap in hand, to bank managers or other lending sources asking for money to begin your writing career. There are no financial risks to take into account. All you need in this business are a few ideas in your head, and the ability to put them down on paper in such a way that an editor cannot resist publishing them, nor readers ignore them. The ideas must usually be put down in some legible form. So, unless you have exceptionally neat and attractive handwriting, your longer manuscripts at least must be typed. Even if you are using computers, faxes or the Internet, the same rule applies.

8 Opportunities for writing are always there. You need never be made redundant. Some of the liveliest Fleet Street writers are still working though they have passed their 70th and 80th birthdays. Printers' ink is in their blood. One magazine folds, another opens. Even if you have a specialism which loses favour temporarily, you can adapt and go into an associated field. This rarely becomes necessary for, as a specialist, you get known in the industry, and there are always outlets for your specialised skills.

Financial journalist Lorna Bourke once said that in spite of all her technical knowledge, if writing about gardening paid more, she would become a gardening expert. This kind of changeover is not possible for expertise (such as medicine) which may take years to acquire, but in other areas, especially those in which the law frequently changes, you can be as good as the next man or woman. If you can read you can write, learn to write, or get someone to write for you.

9 Another advantage of writing for money is the satisfaction it affords the writer. Being paid for your output gives it the stamp of professionalism. In monetary terms, at least, the

30 Ways To Make Money – IN WRITING

reward proves that in a very competitive market place, your work has worth. Do not disregard this angle. Think of the words used by Quigly in Graham Greene's novel, *The Captain and the Enemy*: "Finance," he said, "comes into everything. Politics, war, marriage, crime, adultery. Everything that exists in the world has something to do with money. Even religion. The priest has to buy his bread and wine and the criminal has to buy his gun – or his plane." Get satisfaction from turning out the best you can do: but ensure that your best is suitably rewarded.

10 Lastly, whereas in many professions (such as banking, stockbroking, politics), 'top' women are still few and far between, there is not the same barrier in the writing world. Many of the huge volumes turned out by the pound in the US are written by women, and personal finance sections of UK daily and Sunday newspapers are largely staffed or edited by them. Babies, however, do tend to make at least a hiccup in a career wedded to desk or office. But a writer working at home can have as many or as few babies as she pleases, and providing some organisation is possible, including earmuffs at night (!), the output need not alter, though working hours may have to change.

So the conclusion is that writing for money has so many advantages that, as a profession or as a hobby, it must be taken into account by anybody looking for a few extra shekels or a bit more job satisfaction.

Folow these ten golden rules and you can become a successful writer. Here are thirty ways to do so. . .

The Feature Article

For professionals and beginners alike, the easiest and quickest way to earn money from writing is by the feature article. Over 700 UK newspapers and magazines, ranging from the *Aberdeen Evening Express* to *Zest*, appear in the *Writers' & Artists' Year Book*. With so many outlets, there should be room for your short story, gossip paragraphs, Letters to the Editor, puzzles and so on.

The publications listed appeal to thousands, even millions of different readers, from accountants and animal lovers to yacht owners, cooks and coin collectors to woodworkers and zoologists. They show that there is not a single human activity which cannot form the basis of an article – or a story, play, or film. How to write for these and many other markets, and earn money for doing so, is described in the following pages.

But in all cases, save for music and the visual arts, you start with an idea. For a feature article, that idea has to be translated into words which will inform and/or entertain. Use them intelligently and they will become cash in your pocket. Where do you find ideas? They are all around you, unrecognised assets lying in wait for you to pick up. Get a new viewpoint; see them in a different way. As an example, impeded by three small children, I once clambered on to a No. 8 bus with the grace of an elephant. "Never mind dear," said a very old Cockney, "stock's as good as capital any day." That sentence brought home to me how children were once regarded as security for old age.

Conversations on buses or at bus stops are often germination points for ideas. So are museums and ancient houses with their wonderful exhibits and tales of long ago. Travel enriches the mind, even if it drains your pocket. Newspapers and magazines themselves, particularly if you hope to write for them, can stimulate you into controversy. Try also public relations firms for facts and even stories about products and services that you could write about. The calendar is another starting point: what readers would be interested in the dates mentioned?

Get your idea, hold, and develop it. To do that, you must write it down, otherwise it floats away like thistledown in the wind. After the idea comes the market. Who is most likely to buy your work? Ask this question before you develop your idea into a full length article. Deduce from the contents of the magazine or newspaper which you hope will publish your work, what is most acceptable. You are writing to be published, to earn money for doing so, not as a thesis, or exercise in self expression. Don't send a piece on stamp collecting (unless it depicts locomotives) to the readers of a model railway magazine, or one on model railways to mountain climbers.

Monthly magazines need summer submission for articles on skiing and similar winter topics to allow time for publication; vice versa for summer topics. Professional freelances rarely attempt speculative work – that is sending work before any commitment by the editor to publish has been made. By contrast, a beginner will either have to send the full text or ask a key question.

The question can be merely a request asking if the editor would like an article on this or that subject with your qualifications for doing it; or your submission can be longer, with a title, synopsis and suggested length and a reference to any topicality (anniversary etc.) or other item that might make the piece more saleable. Unless the article is a long one (over 1,000 words) or you are going to be very prolific, it usually makes more sense for a beginner to send the whole text. Skip the opening question and go for the kill.

Aim for the LOOK, YOU, SEE, SO approach. In other words, get hold of the reader in the first paragraph. Stun him or her with such a good opening (LOOK) that he must read on. Then show how the piece is relevant to his particular interests, his problems (YOU). Finally, come out with your conclusion, (SEE) and round up your theme (SO).

Thus, if you are writing about safety in the home, begin with some dramatic example showing how the home is the worst place for accidents. Make this especially relevant to the reader. Give statistics to back up your case. Then suggest how the home can be made safer, this or that hazard avoided. Alternatively, answer the questions *Who, When, What, Why* and possibly *How* which your article will raise in your readers' minds.

Give yourself three possible publications where your work can find an opening, type the manuscript double spacing on A4 paper, unless you prefer a word processor. Not everybody does. I got my first computer over twenty years ago, because I was always altering my manuscript. Now I am a software 'addict.'

Use a phone call to the switchboard of the publishing company to find the name of a specific editor to whom you should send the hard copy of your manuscript and disk (if required). Enclose a stamped addressed envelope for their return if necessary. Keep a photocopy of the manuscript plus a back-up disk. Record where and when you sent your work out as well as noting down items such as phone calls, faxes, stamps, paper, disks, room heat and similar expenses for the Inland Revenue. They can all be offset against tax.

One author boasts of never having received any rejections in a working life, but this situation is so rare as to indicate a most vivid and obviously useful imagination. Far more common are the rejection of countless books which became best sellers. If your work comes back, be not disheartened. All it proves is that your work was not suitable for that outlet at that time. It may suit another publication. Check your article over once more. Was the style right for the paper, chatty or serious, as necessary? Did it get or deserve a big yawn or did you liven it up with quotes; break down the thick wodge of type into more compact paragraphs? Was a mass readership likely to be interested in your particular theme or topic, or did it have only limited appeal? Were there enough facts to back up your ideas, and were they accurate? How was your timing?

If satisfied with your answers, send your manuscript out **again** and **again** until it lands safely. You are unique and so is your work. Have faith in it.

The Religious Press

The religious press offers an easy entry for the beginner. Perhaps because of this, contributors are not exactly handsomely paid. Once after I had interviewed the headmaster of a famous public school, he gave me this tip. "If ever you want to make money from writing," he said, "keep clear of the religious press." He was an ordained priest, so perhaps money had not been his own goal.

But whatever it lacks in terms of payment, the religious press excels in giving writers encouragement and courtesy. Like other commercial organisations, a religious newspaper or magazine has to pay its way or shut up shop. The profit it makes cannot match that of publications with a vast circulation and revenue to match. Freelance fees are therefore much smaller than those that can be earned from the big newspapers. There are certain advantages, however, in writing for the smaller ones.

If your piece falls just short of publication standard, the editor may have time to tell you why: a boon in itself to a beginner.

One of my first ever pieces to a religious newspaper came back "Highly readable and much useful information, but for our readers, not enough point." That criticism was worth a great deal to me. Learning from it that an article needed a theme, a conclusion, I sold my next feature without difficulty.

The second advantage of writing for the religious press is, strange as it may seem, freedom. The article you send in to the *Jewish Chronicle* or a Muslim newspaper, the *Catholic Herald* or the *Universe*, naturally differs from what you would attempt in a magazine for agnostics or Seventh Day Adventists, but within those limitations, editors do allow you the chance to write in your own style and advocate what you wish.

The third advantage of using the religious press is as a starting point. It provides beginners with a market while they are still learning their trade. They do not have to concentrate on religious issues: they can write on practical subjects like cookery, or on social issues like abortion, divorce, the homeless, capital punishment and so on. They can try for the letter pages, short story or news items. Never, for God's sake, preach.

Go for the field that suits you: interviews with Church personalities (check how the various personages are addressed); reporting meetings of interest to Christians, preferably spiced up with a photograph or two which you can get from agencies, or use your own skills in this direction. Here is an editor's tip on 'clerical' photos. "We are not interested in static pictures of bishops or priests, of which we have so many. We much prefer an 'action' picture, for example an interesting close-up of faces listening to the speeches, or a good scenic picture that relates to the congress. I know these are more hard to come by but anything like straight platform pictures are useless to us."

Topicality adds to the acceptability of a feature for the

religious press as elsewhere. Get or make up a calendar listing the feasting/fasting days of the religious group for whom you are writing. Create small biographies of saints or holy people which you can send in to the press on the anniversaries of their births (or deaths). And in a Christian country such as the UK nominally is, the great Christian festivals should provide you with a few ideas.

Another way of earning money from the religious press is by travel articles. Famous shrines, areas of pilgrimage, places where holy people have lived or worked will all find interested editors and readers. Photos, even if the editor does not use them, will make the article more acceptable in his eyes. Don't write from a sectarian angle, but emphasise the attractions of the place, with facts about the cost of hotels, transport, amenities.

If your article does not get accepted by your first choice, there are many journals, other than religious ones, which take travel articles. You therefore give yourself the chance of three markets instead of one. Indeed, in your manuscript book, you should note down at least three markets where your work might sell.

Helping out your parish or community by contributing or even editing a newsletter is more likely to make you poorer rather than richer, but you might be offered the loan of an office and/or typewriter/duplicator, useful if you have none of your own. You will also learn additional skills, and local news and views which can be saleable in one form or another.

By contrast with the small rewards for articles and news pieces, larger works of religious interest can really hit the jackpot. One has only to think of titles like Graham Greene's *The Heart of the Matter*, Audrey Erskine Lindop's *The Singer Not the Song*, and that fascinating oddity *The Name of The Rose*. For the battle between faith and power there is *Vatican* by Malachi Martin: not quite bedtime reading unless you're prepared to risk paralysis of the arm by holding up its weight.

As a bonus there are the awards made by various bodies for religious writing. The H. H. Wingate/*Jewish Quarterly* awards £4,000 annually for a work of fiction or non fiction submitted by publishers which stimulates interest in themes of Jewish concern, and a further £1,000 for an unpublished work of poetry. Details PO Box 1148, London, NW5 2AZ (0171 485 4062).

HarperCollins offer a £2,000 biennial award for a book submitted by publishers which has made the most distinguished contribution to the relevance of Christianity in the modern world by a living citizen of the British Commonwealth, the Republic of Ireland or South Africa (for details, 'phone 0181 741 7070).

So the message is clear: If you can write forcibly and sincerely about moral problems, human conduct and belief, describe credible characters and weave interesting plots against a religious background, then you are in line for rich rewards on earth and maybe in a life to come. Can there be any better inspiration for the 'religious' writer than that?

Business Communication

Business communication covers a large field, and gives scope for many kinds of writing skill. Reports, publicity articles, brochures, instruction manuals and translations are all needed, and much can be done by freelances.

The first requirement of business communication, rarely achieved, is that sender and receiver should understand the message. Both parties have to know what, who and how. For economic or political reports, or for those going to members of an organisation such as a trade union or Chamber of Commerce, when and why might also be essential. The consequences of not being in command of these essentials of good business communication could be a disastrous strike, the loss of good employee/employer relations and/or a fall in company profits. Wrong instructions can also involve dire consequences for producer and consumer.

Having mastered subject matter, audience and the medium used to give out information, where does the writer wanting to make some money in business communication begin? Annual reports issued by companies do not afford much opportunity. They are concerned with the accounts, balance sheets, profit and loss of the company and are targeted mainly at shareholders and brokers, though they may contain some snippets of information about promotions and new developments.

Newsletters distributed or sent to employees are usually more lively, with items about products and personalities. To write regularly for these, it is necessary to have access to people in the various departments and to know what's going on.

If your work is liked, you might be asked to do more. Quite often, vacancies for producing these magazines on a part time or fee paying basis are advertised in the Media Appointments pages of the national newspapers, particularly *The Guardian*.

You will be responsible for seeing the paper to bed, to get it printed and produced. Don't be afraid of tackling something new. In the journalistic world, there is always somebody ready to help. Unlike the world of management where you always first say 'no', and then maybe relent, to earn money in writing you always first say 'yes', and then maybe repent.

Some reports investigate a problem in depth, with recommendations for its solution. These reports do not generally arise from the initiative of an individual writer but at the request of a department or body of interested people. If you learn that such a group is about to be set up, and you have a contribution to make, contact the leading figures or organisation concerned. Your offer may be accepted and used, but not always paid for, as it will be considered made for the good of society (not the payment usually offered to those who head the report). You get expenses for attending and, from private organisations, some recompense.

Most money in business communication for outsiders can

usually be earned in writing promotional literature. Companies bring out pamphlets and brochures, explaining how superior their product or service is compared with others. These brochures may be handled by agencies with their own designers.

Write to the marketing manager of the company if you have some particular knowledge of the product or service, or to public relations firms giving your background and what your writing can achieve for the firm. Approach large firms such as the financial organisations, and others who may be bringing out products and services ahead of some new legislation, such as going into Europe, pensions, or taxation. Promotional writing, if you can get it, is extremely well paid, higher than many national dailies, but you need to have a high standard of writing ability, professional expertise, and speed. When time is of the essence, you must work to strict deadlines.

Another good writing opportunity arises out of press campaigns such as those for or against new roads, or animal rights and environmental issues. Where you won't find much chance of earning money from companies is when any current campaign is likely to hit their sales. Examples might be the banning of advertisements for products such as cigarettes or alcohol. To earn anything in this situation, look at alternatives: companies, for example, that are producing alcohol free beers and lagers. They want to persuade customers that the new products are as good as those previously consumed but which are now considered a health hazard.

Instruction manuals are another form of business communication, rather like an extension of the How To. . . sector of writing. Break down the instructions into a series of steps. Getting the right sequence is very important and one of the dangers of this kind of writing is to assume the reader knows too much.

You could therefore write instructions for the use of a medicament, telling in the most simple language when and how it should be taken, without saying what appears to you to be obvious, namely first remove the wrapping. Better to assume your reader is a moron than risk this kind of mistake.

Instruction manuals need good indexing, particularly for those relating to computers. One doesn't want to wade through several pages to find out how to change from double to single spacing, or how to alter the tab key. Often the 'help' key, very good for abstruse problems, is no help at all for word processing.

If you are so busy writing (you should be so lucky) and have no time to index a manual, apply for help to the Society of Indexers (0171 916 7809). If you aren't busy and think you could do a good job of indexing for others, you might ask to go on their list yourself. Pay is not high, but you could be in line for the Library Association's (0171 636 7543) Wheatley medal (see Competitions And Awards, page 41) presented for an outstanding index originated and published in the UK in the preceding three years.

Products and services today encircle the globe, so translations are an important part of business communication and of instruction manuals. You usually need some technical knowledge about an industry (gold, oil, banking, engineering) or a product. Try first one of the agencies that specialise in translations; if unsuccessful, start up on your own.

An esoteric language, strangely, may be far more useful than French or German where there are already so many fluent linguists. Any skill, such as in computers, accountancy or nursing, will give you an extra advantage.

Biography

It is possible to produce a good biography, even if you have never had a line published. This category of non fiction is very much alive though you are unlikely to get the huge fees paid for biographies such as that of Bernard Shaw, or Richard Ellman's *Oscar Wilde*.

These and similar works are usually the result of years of research, and sometimes privileged information, but simple stories like that of Christabel, an English girl married to a German in Nazi Germany, may make a big impact and be adapted for TV. You don't have to be an historian to write a life story. The facts are usually there for the asking and a bit of research.

To create readable biography, emphasise the significant incidents in a person's life; what changed their ideas; how they coped with disaster, success, tragedy. Begin with a synopsis of the life story you mean to write and complete a specimen chapter. Check whether your proposed book will fit into a series. Check also with current biographies in the library or booksellers and send your completed effort to the publishers who, judging by the books they produce, are most likely to be interested in your work.

A good exercise before you start your biography proper is to read the lives of other writers. Their trials and failures will often provide you with encouragement, help you realise how much some authors sacrifice to pursue their aims, and what interests readers about the way they lived and worked.

Begin with a short story, *The Art of Biography*, by the 1987 Booker prizewinner Penelope Lively, in her collection *Pack of Cards*. The opening tells you the preparation a biographer makes before writing a word. It is also an excellent example of the short story by a leading exponent of the art.

Then take a look at real lives: Eugene O'Neill, for example. His brother James died in a sanatorium. His oldest son left two wives and committed suicide in his thirties. Eugene's daughter, Oona, married at 18 years against his wishes the 54 year old film star Charles Chaplin.

Eugene's son by his second wife tragically lost a child at only two months, became incapable of work and had to live on the legacy his wife had inherited from her mother (murdered by her stepfather.) The ex-husband of Eugene's third and last wife, Carlotta Monterey, committed suicide within three days of the pair arriving back in the States from a long stay abroad.

Would a history like that compensate you for creating *Mourning Becomes Electra?* Eugene O'Neill's life has all the ingredients for a successful biography. So has that of Edgar Wallace, illegitimate son of small time actress Polly Richards. His energy was prodigious, as can be seen by one weekend spent at his country house, Chalklands. Beginning on Friday night and finishing by 9am on Monday, he dictated a full length novel of 80,000 saleable words about Charles Peace, called *The Devil Man*. Could you even do that in a year?

Biography

Have you enjoyed reading *Dubliners* or other works by James Joyce? Then delve into that most sympathetic life of him written by his brother Stanislaus. If you ever feel your English needs improving, read the biography of Joseph Conrad, the Polish seaman who learnt English as a second language. The days when he found himself unable to write brought him to an abyss of despair from which he was rescued only by the practical realism of his wife Jessie.

And if your first (for you will surely write others) biography comes back, and the only money you see in writing is that spent on stamps, think of Evan Hunter. He could find no editorial work after searching for months, became a telephone seller of lobsters, sent manuscripts regularly all over the United States, without a single acceptance until Scott Meredith's Literary Agency in which he finally found a job sold one of his stories for $12.60. His novels later commanded thousands before he even put pen to paper.

You have nothing to lose but your stamps, so have a shot at a life story NOW!

Writing For Children

At first glance, writing for a children's market seems easy. Anybody can do it, and everybody does. That is why the competition is enormous and selling so aggressive. But the rewards, if you are successful, are enormous too. You have only to think of names like Enid Blyton, Malcolm Saville or Arthur Ransome; characters like Paddington Bear, The Railway Children, The Wombles of Wimbledon, Biggles and Just William, to realise that children's stories go on for much longer than their counterparts in popular adult fiction.

There are also the subsidiary rights. These include adaptations and films like Roald Dahl's *Danny, The Champion of the World* (though films more often arise from adult books), and the production of toys, clothes, badges and similar spin-offs. If you find the right touch in writing for children, and can keep up your output, you will get a following of loyal readers and an income for life. Furthermore, new generations will be coming along for your books, though they will be younger each year.

The market includes animal stories, adventure, young

romance and science fiction, to name but a few. So how do you enter this possibly lucrative field? First try your hand at anything: stories, articles, rhymes, things to make and do (activities), puzzles. To make money out of writing for children, you must write much and often, until you hit the jackpot. These early efforts tell you what sells most readily. Write to editors of local newspapers and 'give-aways' asking them if they would like a children's page or column. Send a sample of your work.

Get copies of the magazines, papers or comics for which you wish to write (publishers often supply free copies and even a few hints on the material they want). Comic strips sometimes need writers to provide simple dialogue for filling the 'balloons'. Adult magazines sometimes also have a children's section for short bright stories, snippets of interesting information and things to make and do.

When you have gained a little experience, or even before if you are madly keen to start on something longer, try a children's book, or a TV/radio script. The big advantage that children's novels have over the adult kind is in length. There are no huge tomes, save encyclopaedias, published specifically for children. You can range from a few pages, well illustrated, sometimes with pullouts or cutouts, to 35,000 or even 60,000 words if you wish. Few children's novels come larger than that.

Contrary to the usual situation, women with children have an advantage over other potential writers because their 'copy' is all around them. They need never struggle to get the right dialogue, only to get the time to transcribe the copy.

Provide action and conflict. Characters are of lesser importance, tending to represent goodies and baddies rather than real life people – though there are brilliant exceptions.

Writing simply, essential for children's books, is a wonderful discipline. You constantly have to search for an easy word instead of the more difficult one that comes readily to mind. Eschew complex sentences. (Eschew is the type of word you wouldn't use in a children's book without good reason.) As an example of simple writing, so lucid that it almost glows, read *The Happy Prince and Other Stories* by the so gifted but so luckless Oscar Wilde for his sons. It was reissued by Penguin to celebrate their 60 years in publishing, in one of the small Penguins at 60p.

As your book proceeds you may forget or ignore the age group for whom you are writing. Watch any tendency for dialogue to grow a little 'older', sentences longer. Don't allow your characters overlong 'thoughts'. Use a sentence to reveal ideas, then translate them into deeds. Moral dilemmas differ from those of the adult world where great themes create philosophical discussion between the protagonists. Children learn more easily by action and example, from books as well as life. But the wonderful children's series by C. S. Lewis, beginning with *The Lion, The Witch and The Wardrobe,* relate far more than simple action.

Be careful with facts. On this point (and others) H. G. Wells, who was a very hard taskmaster, wrote some good advice about a proposed book, *The Science of Life,* on which he was collaborating with Sir Julian Sorrell Huxley (brother of Aldous). Don't leave God the Father (Wells was here referring modestly to himself), he told his collaborator, to look up facts. The conversion of millimetres into inches or of degrees (C) was not his job. Wells added another bit of advice equally relevant for all authors, telling Huxley not to send him "bad, patchy typing" for "you are getting enough out of the job to get the typewriting properly done and in time".

Be careful, therefore, with facts. If you cannot verify them, don't put them in. When you are writing children's non fiction books say on stamps, or coins, or football, ensure to the best of your ability that your data is accurate and up to date.

An outlet that appears to be widening is in providing odd or interesting information catalogued for easy reference, like the *Guinness Book of Records,* or pictorial facts in a weekly column. Another opportunity comes with writing for a series: publishers who bring out a series of 'nature' books will need writers with some knowledge of birds and beasts; others may want biographers of 'heroes' in football or sport. Watch out for these titles. Note those in preparation. Then write to the publishers and suggest ideas of your own to fit in with the series. In most books for children, a synopsis and two or three chapters are enough to show whether your work is suitable for their imprint.

Even if you don't make a fortune from writing for children, you will learn much by entering the market. Don't be a slave to current fashion. Keep your integrity. Think of the children who will spend their own pocket money to buy your work. It is the highest of accolades, so ensure that they gain pleasure and extend the boundaries of their imagination by what you have written.

Competitions And Awards

You may never achieve fame, never become a millionaire from your writing, never qualify for the Booker Prize (£20,000 plus all the hype and sales that go with it). Take heart. Graham Greene never got what he so richly deserved, namely the Nobel Prize for Literature. He still continued to be a best seller and, better still, a great writer.

As a scribbler, to use Nigel Lawson's memorable noun, you will probably not achieve the fame and glory of a Nobel prizewinner, but there are many other awards that may come your way. That you have not yet had a word published should not deter you. Instead it should spur you on to enter literary competitions and hope that somebody will be perspicacious enough to award a prize for your memorable prose (or poetry). Get the leaflet (SAE) from the Book Trust, 45 East Hill, Wandsworth SW18 2QZ, on awards and grants for **writers.** Their book, *Literary Prizes and Awards* (£4.99) has a bigger content but covers also awards for works submitted by **publishers,** which is unlikely to be of great help to writers unless they are in the final throes of giving birth to a literary epic.

Meanwhile, the competitions provide motivation when you are finding it hard to get started: with ideas, opening lines or plots. By entering a short story competition, you will at least get practice in writing and marketing your wares.

Ruth Atkinson was launched on her writing career by winning a *Woman's Own* short story competition in 1988. Eight years later, she became the winner of the Whitbread Book of the Year Award with her first novel *Behind The Scenes At The Museum,* beating two outstanding candidates: Salman Rushdie's *The Moor's Last Sigh* and Lord Jenkins' biography of Gladstone. The Booker Prize, too, was won by a woman with *The Ghost Road* by Pat Barker, the first year ever since their inception that both prizes were won by women. And the Orange Prize launched in 1996 (and to be awarded in 1996) is another prize on the stocks for women. Anonymously endowed, it is worth £30,000 and open to women of any age or country, for a work published in Britain on any subject.

In some competitions, there may even be consolation prizes for 'losers'. The magazine *She* once ran a 2,000 word story competition in conjunction with Timotei Shampoo. In addition to a large first prize and several further ones, every entrant got a towel, shampoo and conditioner as a consolation for not being among the 'firsts'.

Many competitions not offered on a regular basis occasionally appear in a newspaper or magazine. The *Daily Mail* sometimes features one for the best introduction to a story in not more than 200 words. The winning author also gets the chance of having his or her work published as a full length novel.

The Observer, The *Daily Telegraph* and *Woman* magazine

occasionally run similar short story competitions as do the free journals issued to passengers on aircraft. If you are seeking competition prizes but are, let us say, modest about your literary talent, have a go at the easier puzzles set occasionally by building societies or those on the labels of grocery packets and tins. Trying to solve puzzles, to write captions or slogans keeps you alert and one day you may be happily surprised (as I was) by the postman bringing you a bottle of champagne for naming the right authors in a 'Who said that?' competition, or a camera for devising the best caption for an almost unintelligible picture.

Slogans and tie breaks are often required when there are several correct entries. Not all of the prizes are in cash; they may be TVs or holidays abroad, cars, new kitchens etc. But they come tax free and are an honest way of obtaining consumer goods without cost.

For lengthier and more 'literary' competitions, look elsewhere. The categories include: general, fiction, non fiction, academic works, biography and autobiography, Christian, crime, essays, a first work, history, historical novels, romance, plays, poetry, reference, science fiction, short stories, translation and travel. Over 200 are listed by the Book Trust but check with the organisers that the rules of their competitions have not changed since the list went to press.

The Somerset Maugham Awards (three of £5,000–£6,000 each) offered annually by the Society of Authors, 84 Drayton Gardens SW10 9SB, for British subjects under 35 years, must be submitted by **publishers;** so too must another prize for young people under 35 years, namely the *Mail on Sunday*–John Llewellyn Rhys Prize of £5,000.

Greater chances for the new writer come from WH Smith

(Public Relations, 7 Holbein Place, London SW1W 8NR) with their competitions and promotions. In their Young Writers' Competition they offer awards for the best poems or prose by anyone in the UK under 17 (three age groups). Prizes total more than £7,000 for schools and individuals, with the latter having their work included in a paperback every year.

WH Smith also organise promotions for published books such as the Mind-Boggling books for children (£5,000 prize) selected by children; the Fresh Talent promotion: no cash prizes but promotion of six titles from 100–150 first novels selected by the Retail team, and the Thumping Good Read Award of £5,000 founded in 1992 for the best new fiction of the year as judged by a panel of customers.

The Arts Councils (among them the Northern, Southern, Eastern) have their own regional awards sometimes open only to residents within the districts served or covering stories set in those backgrounds. Occasionally bursaries or grants are donated by legacy or gift to 'deserving' writers living in or setting their stories in the neighbourhood. Enquire at the Leisure and Amenities Services at your local library.

Residents/natives of Scotland, Wales and Ireland, or writers who choose those countries for their settings, may be eligible for the *Irish Times* Literary Prizes; the Dublin Literary Award or The Scottish Arts Council's bursaries of £3,000–£8,000 each for 'professional writers'. The Tir N-og Awards for Welsh fiction include short stories and picture books.

For more details of regular annual and biennial prizes and awards covering other specialisms, see the section on Prizes and Awards in *The Writers' & Artists' Yearbook* or *The Writer's Handbook. The Guide to Literary Prizes, Grants and Awards in Britain and Ireland*, compiled by the Book Trust and the Society of Authors, gives the categories of awards (biography, children, fiction, short stories, history, illustrative journalism, non fiction, poetry and drama, publishing and printing, religious, specialist and translations) with the amount of prize money, addresses for entries and closing dates.

Sponsored by Whitaker Bibliographic Services, the Library Association (7 Ridgmount Street WC1E 7AE) makes awards for works of reference including bibliography and, with the Society of Indexers, for 'an outstanding index published in the United Kingdom'. Whitakers are prizewinning publishers of Bookbank: it lists Books in Print on CD Rom, so could be helpful to computer buffs. (Martin Whitaker, 12 Dyott Street WC1A 1DF.)

'Attachments' are sometimes set up in a particular community or educational establishment to help writers financially while they are getting established. Fellowships may be created to encourage a prizewinner's own writing, or writers' workshops established.

The Royal Literary Fund and the Society of Authors have details of grants for impoverished or disabled writers. Join a Writers' Circle or similar organisation (addresses in your local library) to get details of updated and new awards, conferences, courses and competitions for authors.

Journalism has its own competitions and awards. It may seem difficult to compete with expert editors and staff writers, but freelance writers have more time and often scoop the awards. Texaco offers prizes of £750 in each of nine industrial sectors for the "best reporting of the issues and stories concerning industry, business, management and people at work". The company also makes special awards which focus on such subjects as energy, science and technology. Other organisations offering prizes to journalists include the British Insurance and Investment Brokers' Association (BIIBA) tel: 0171 623 9043. They offer Journalist of the Year Awards in the following sections: consumer/broadsheet; consumer/tabloid; technical-news and technical-research) and range from the highly commended (£50) to £500 for journalists who make the "greatest overall contribution to the insurance and investment industries through their reporting".

Bradford and Bingley Building Society also offer prizes for financial reporting. So too do Alexander Clay & Partners Consulting. Their two main awards to Pension and Investment journalists (consumer and technical) are based on the submission of four published articles (or broadcasts) of which two must be on pensions. The winners receive cheques for £1,200 and a permanent memento. Two runners up receive £350 each. The prizes are usually presented by an MP or other august personage.

The winners and high 'losers' are usually invited to a lunch in the House of Commons. Journalists' prizes occasionally go to the Absolute Beginner. In my first year of writing on financial topics, I was lucky enough to be the runner up in the Insurance Consumer section to the then Personal Finance Editor of *The Sunday Times*, Diana Wright, and a newcomer can't hope for much higher than that.

Look out for the competitions advertised in your newspapers and local library. They provide motivation when you may be on a downbeat. It is also interesting to read the winners and wonder, for this is not always obvious, what they have that you didn't.

Letters

An easy way into print is to write a letter to the editor – or so it may seem. But letters, too, must have a special appeal, otherwise they won't get read, acted upon or published. The big difference between letters and other forms of writing is that they are more personal. They create a one-to-one situation and can act as a double edged weapon.

A spoken word is soon forgotten, a written one may live long after its author. So ask yourself before your letter goes off whether you are prepared for your correspondence to be bruited around. Even a letter marked personal may have more than one audience: for example, the immediate recipient, and others whose impact could be more important.

An unhappy example of this 'whirlpool' effect is the famous Bywaters murder case. Edith Thompson wrote to Frederick Bywaters, a 20 year old clerk employed on the P&O Liners, who was infatuated by her. One day, he came home, met Mrs. Thompson and her husband in an Ilford street, and stabbed her 32 year old husband to death.

Edith Thompson had not helped with the act, and did not know of it in advance. But in her letters to Bywaters, which he had unfortunately kept, she discussed the use of poison and powdered glass, perhaps in an imaginative way like a crime story, without meaning any real harm to her husband. Those letters proved her death warrant. Rene Weiss who wrote about her in the book *Criminal Justice* was given access to the Home Office files, but one, explaining why Edith Thompson never got reprieved in spite of a million signatures for clemency, was missing.

This unhappy story arose out of letters used in evidence against an accused person. They went beyond the bounds of the one-to-one situation which a letter creates. Their contents were acted upon by others who were never meant to see them. Romances as well as crimes have grown out of letters, and many writers use the medium of letters to tell a story. Read these authors if you want to make money from your own letter writing skills. (In some parts of the world, this is a paid occupation.)

There is *Daddy Long Legs* by Jean Webster, still going strong after 40 years. Richard Sherman and William Hazlitt Upson also used the letter writing format in their short stories. One excellent example is *Simple Arithmetic* by Virginia Moriconi, first published in Transatlantic Review 1963 and reprinted in *Best American Short Stories 3*. The characters of child, father, mother and stepmother are beautifully sketched with hardly a descriptive line, while the ending conveys a wealth of meaning and a real understanding of a child's world.

Letters helped develop the extraordinary love story of the Brownings. Elizabeth, an invalid poet, is immured in her room. Robert, many years her junior, reads and is moved by her poems. He writes to her and gets invited to her home, an accomplishment in itself.

They send notes to each other. Romance blossoms rapidly. Aided by a faithful servant, Elizabeth escapes from a tyrannical father, marries Robert in a local church and elopes with him to Italy where she has a son and they all live happily ever after – or at least until her death. Too good to be true? Read the letters and see.

Equally enlightening is the correspondence of Frieda von Richthofen to D. H. Lawrence. Lawrence, the schoolmaster son of a Nottinghamshire miner, meets Frieda, the rich wife of a professor teaching in England, and is stunned (but obviously impressed) by her inability to turn on the gas tap to boil water in her own home. (This was a chore done by servants.) The incongruous pair fell in – and out – of love but remained married throughout their various traumas and his ill health. Their romance is told in her letters.

Florence Nightingale's correspondence is quite different, revealing an administrator with an exceptional grasp of detail. She wrote her letters to influence friends in Parliament at a time when women could not act directly in the political or economic field. Because she framed her words so well, she achieved more for the soldiers (and ultimately the women who worked for her) than the commanders in the field.

Lady Hamilton could not spell. This proved no handicap in her letters, and may even have furthered her romance with Nelson. More modern are the letters between New England aristocrat Edith Wharton and Morton Fullerton, the man with whom, at the age of 45, she fell in love. Touching, too, is the correspondence between Bill Cook, a Second World War padre, and Helen, the sweetheart he left behind, published 40 years later as *Khaki Parish, Our War... Our Love*.

Letters revive happy or painful memories, act as a history source book, a compendium of style, a method of telling a story, a money spinner, or even as evidence in a court case.

They can be *appealing,* in which you ask for something; *placatory,* when you try to soothe the savage breast of an irate customer or reader; *denouncing,* where you complain about the machine that doesn't work, the commodity that has proved unsatisfactory, the bad service you got, the bus or train that arrived late or didn't turn up at all. Finally, there is the *stating* letter, in which you give information, though not always as a recital of facts.

Any of these letters can bring you a monetary reward, but as they have different aims, they must be phrased in different ways. If you are appealing, you are trying to elicit a response, to ask for something, whereas when you state a fact, you merely draw attention to that fact. The monetary reward may be indirect: your money back on a purchase, a replacement holiday or goods, a job interview which boosts your salary or enhances your promotion prospects.

Newspapers and women's magazines often publish prize letters, including a larger sum for the best of the week. These letters need to have something special: topicality, unique or unusual experiences, different life styles. The financial section of The *Mail on Sunday* sometimes runs competitions in conjunction with other organisations such as the Royal Mail, for the best business letters, how to deal with an irate customer and so on. Prizes are usually business oriented, for example software or computers.

In women's magazines, a few compliments will not come amiss, so if you have been a reader since the first issue, say so. If not, read two or three copies of the paper or magazine, and study the letters that have been printed. Then write one yourself. You have nothing to lose but your time and your stamp.

The Free Press

The free press is not quite what it sounds. It refers to newspapers delivered free of charge to your door. Give-away newspapers reflect the development of mail order business whereby people are persuaded, or not, to buy goods illustrated in the brochures or pamphlets that come through the letter box.

Free newspapers vary in size from 4 to 8 pages, but are sometimes much larger with property and other supplements. Depending on the locality covered, many can also have a big circulation. They may go into over 100,000 homes and be read by an even larger number of households. The papers are usually distributed by teams of housewives, pensioners and students who are paid for covering an area or 'posting' 1,000 copies.

How can the proprietors afford to send out these 'freebies'? The answer is simply revenue from advertisers. Most of the articles published (but not all) are linked to the advertisements carried in the paper. As an example, I was asked to write 1,500 words on the opening of a new extension to a Health Food shop in the area.

I interviewed the owner, got information about him (age, background, family), his most popular selling lines, and about the new premises (area, cost, mortgage). My piece was published in a middle page spread with pictures of the proprietor and his new shop premises alongside.

Further adverts, on health foods and similar products, were featured on other pages. The owner of the shop and the other advertisers paid the newspaper proprietor for his space. In effect, though I reported only the facts, the editor was paying me to do a kind of public relations job for the Health Food shop, and other advertisers of a like nature.

Many other commissions of this kind later came my way. Frequent and well paid, they made a welcome addition to the household budget. Some arose out of new Housing Acts, and legislation affecting improvement grants. The editor saw that most of his advertisements were from builders, DIY shops, plumbing, roofing and glazing specialists. He therefore plugged the grants for all he was worth – not to help the local citizenry to better housing (though he may have been sincerely glad to do so), but to attract advertising.

The give-away press has grown bigger still since those days. Instead of one paper, two come into my door each week. Such papers offer the chance that few other publications provide in quite the same way, to make money by writing for them. Study those that are delivered to your house, see what attracts the biggest advertising (usually cars and property), then send in a query to the editor, asking whether he would like you to cover some story that has local relevance, and will enable him and you to earn a bob or two. If the editor likes your idea, he will tell you to go ahead, and often give you some useful tips on how to develop it.

With this type of article, do not neglect to discuss payment. Writing a 1,000 word article at home is different from spending days tracking down background information only to get a rejection slip for your efforts. Take your courage in both hands and ask the editor if there is a 'kill' fee if he doesn't like your finished piece. A 'kill' fee is a kind of consolation prize when a commissioned article cannot be published for reasons beyond the editor's control. If he says not, at least you know where you are and how much time you can afford to spend on a speculative piece.

Another way to begin is to send a controversial letter, which may arouse sufficient interest for you to follow up with a short article on the same subject. Or you can suggest ideas which are a form of advertising such as writing up the restaurants in the area. Even if you only get some free wining and dining for your efforts, it pays for your supper and is all grist to the writer's mill.

During the summer months, articles on any aspect of weddings become acceptable because these can be geared to adverts from caterers, photographers, dress hire and a whole range of other products of interest to brides, grooms, relatives and friends.

In the winter there are floods, insurance, double glazing and insulating materials. Brush up on any specialism you have. Write it as simply as you know how, but always with the prospective reader in mind. So, if you've got an economics degree, don't provide an analysis of Keynes's theory of employment. Tell readers how they can make the most of their money, avoid debt, increase their non taxable income, etc.

If the editor thinks your work will attract his readers' interest, and therefore advertisers, he will look favourably on further articles you send in, or suggestions you make. His tastes are among the most catholic of all editors. He cannot pay Fleet Street rates, but he does give the beginner the option of a wide range of possible features.

There are just two disadvantages in writing for give-aways. You cannot be sure that they are going to continue. Some are owned by large combines, others published almost on a shoestring. Unlike the national dailies or the big publishing houses, they may fold up almost without warning, and your pieces with them.

The second difficulty is that you obviously cannot condemn the product(s) or services about which you are writing. You are purblind, seeing only the good. If you are aiming to be an 'investigative' or 'campaigning' journalist, the give-away press is no place to start.

But it offers, as few other openings do, the chance of well paid and often regular sales, the experience of knowing what editors want, the joy of seeing your name in print, perhaps for the first time, and the confidence to try your luck elsewhere.

The Education Market

Readers' needs can be summed up under five headings. The first is *spiritual:* the need to find some sort of ethic as a basis for living. Alexander Solzhenitsyn's *Cancer Ward* is a good example of a book dealing with this theme. Other needs include the *social* ones, covering human relationships, work, love, marriage, parenting, the environment; *physical:* understanding and care of the body, sex, food, sport, shelter, beauty; *emotional:* a desire for amusement, mystery, drama, entertainment. Finally readers want *mental stimulation:* learning for its own sake; exercising the mind; acquiring skills or crafts; developing a hobby.

Though these needs overlap, all of them provide writers with a vast store of ideas for articles and books. One of the largest, and sometimes the easiest sector to break into, is a reader's need for mental stimulation, for knowledge, for education. This market is so vast that it is best broken down into two parts. The first covers education: books and articles which provide information of a general or cultural kind. The second part of the education market is dealt with in the chapter on text books. And there is a third market briefly mentioned in the chapter *Why Writing?*, namely getting information electronically. Such data is not intended for a long browse, however.

Articles, and especially books that inform, grow from the need to discover certain facts. There appears to be nothing suitable around. Perceive that gap, and you will earn at least a stipend by filling it. How do you fill it? You collect, research, group and write the relevant information for the specific need. You should possess a logical mind and that most underrated of all writing skills: the ability to précis – intelligibly.

As examples of the informative book, several stand out. The first, because it has lasted so long, is Roget's *Thesaurus*. If you are among the few who have never dived into this treasury to pick out a gold nugget, beg or borrow it now. The thesaurus gives alternatives to every kind of noun, verb, adjective and adverb in the English language, as well as phrases in common use.

Nobody who works with words can afford to be without this wonderful work, which first appeared in 1852 and is still going strong. The author's grandson drew royalties on it during his lifetime, and when he died in 1952 (before the UK inflation of the seventies deprived figures of their meaning), he left house and property worth £98,000.

Fowler's *Modern English Usage* covers points of grammar in great detail. It is sometimes amusing, sometimes abstruse – another long-time 'seller' of information, having first come out in 1925. Its annual sales for years topped the 20,000 mark. For me, Fowler's analyses do not make obvious enough what is the right use and the wrong one. Longman's have a newer version, *Guide to English Usage*.

The *Guinness Book of Records* is another example of a book which provides information in an interesting and accessible way. In 1954, Sir Hugh Beaver, managing director of the brewery firm of Guinness, could find no reference book or encyclopaedia on the fastest, largest, smallest. . . on record. Other extremes that might also be wanted were equally hard to find. Sir Hugh had discovered that gap in the 'educational' market which provides writers with the opportunity to sell their skills.

He was introduced to twin brothers Norris and Ross McWhirter, who had their own research agency. They became editors of the *Guinness Book of Records*. First published in 1955, it gives details of record breaking events, people, animals and similar data and, with the exception of the Bible, is the fastest non fiction seller in the world. Published in 14 countries and 10 languages, it is updated annually.

Similar publications which educate and inform their readers include such works as Brewer's *Dictionary of Phrase And Fable*, Halliwell's *Film Guide, The Oxford Companion to English Literature* (editor: Margaret Drabble), three books from Longman: *Music (the Opera Handbook); Dance;* and *All that Jazz*.

Music lovers also have *The Oxford Companion to Music*, by Dr. Percy Scholes. This monumental work about music and musicians contains more than a million words and over 100,000 illustrations. It is in constant demand by musicians, students and libraries throughout the world. The knowledge and experience derived from writing this book helped Dr. Scholes to write another. He completed the *Listener's Guide to Music* in only ten days. How long would it take you to do your own thing? Begin now.

For chess lovers, there is that amazing book by David

Spanier, *Total Chess,* and it **is** total, giving information on every aspect of chess that you can think of, and many that you can't. No wonder it has gone into so many editions. Similar, but without David Spanier's inimitable style, is *The Complete Chess Addict* by Mike Fox and Richard James.

In the field of providing information there is a special niche for young readers. Many specialised publishers bring out books which give light hearted (but authoritative) information to children about the world they live in. Your best chance of publication is in series that are coming out such as *The Book of The Sea,* or *The Shore...* or *Trees* etc.

If you have any artistic ability at all send sketches with your stories. One often sells the other. Think how interwoven are the lovely stories and illustrations in the children's books by Tim Ardizzone, or Paul Gallico *(The Snow Goose).* Don't let the fact that you are not a Beatrix Potter dissuade you, however, from entering the 'information' market for children. Of one thing you may be sure: they will certainly tell you the truth about yourself as a writer.

Summing up, the steps needed to break into the education market are to:

- study publishers' lists
- think of a title that will fit in with the publisher's forthcoming output
- make a synopsis of your proposed book with three fully written chapters
- give the total number of words in the book on your title sheet, that is the sheet which prefaces your work, with your name and address

- suggest a target audience

- give details of your background if relevant (for example, Professor of Botany if your book is labelled *The Flora of the Samarian Coast*), send enough stamps for the return of the manuscript. The publisher didn't ask to see it, so do him the courtesy of a return stamp

Finally, do not forget the new areas of getting and giving information for research or publicity via the Internet.

Text Books

The first step to writing a text book is the same as that for an informative one, namely to perceive a gap in the market. As an example, shortly after I began teaching economics to bankers, I saw that the students had no recommended text book for the compulsory new examination of monetary economics. I outlined a book proposal with three specimen chapters, sent it to a couple of publishers: no luck whatsoever.

The following year, when a book on the subject came out, I was sure my chances of authorship had gone forever. At the same time, however, some publishers' handouts arrived at the college soliciting work from lecturers. This is one method by which publishers find possible new authors. It also provides a way for teachers to earn a secondary income and gives a chance to academics whose promotion might depend on published work. I filled in one of the forms and surprise, surprise, my proposal was taken up and the book published in the next 12 months, four years after my original idea. The lesson to be learnt from this experience is that timing is important not only in topical articles, but even in text book publishing.

Look out not only for a gap in the market, but changes in a syllabus or entry qualifications. Are new exams being proposed?

30 Ways To Make Money – IN WRITING

Has there been an increase in the number of pupils taking the old ones? Such situations provide opportunities for the text book writer. And the rewards can be great. An average novel may sell not much more than 3,500–5,000 copies, whereas even an average text book can go into several editions.

Income can be further boosted by tape recordings, or other aids to learning, so that subsidiary earnings may also exceed that of the novelist. Sometimes books without covers are used as learning material in areas off the beaten track. One of my children's novels, *The Mystery of the Blue Tomatoes,* was distributed in this way for aborigine children in the outbacks of Australia. The writer is paid a percentage for these publications, too.

Ronald Ridout, a young schoolmaster dissatisfied with the English book he was using in the classroom, decided to create a better one. He produced *English Today* which has sold over five million copies; his English Language schoolbooks are also best sellers. Charles Eckersley, a teacher in a polytechnic catering for large numbers of foreign students, saw how great was the need for a text book to help them learn English. He produced *Essential English for Foreign Students.*

The moral is if you want to get a text book out: 'mind the gap' as they say on the London Underground. Teachers are in a particularly fortunate position to know what is wanted, though some of the committees responsible for deciding what a new curriculum is to be, or how an old one doesn't meet current needs, may have odd ideas.

Thus in 1988, a Curriculum committee banned Enid Blyton from primary schools, along with several other childhood favourites, because her work was regarded as sexist and racist. Without wishing to offend the sensitivities of religious belief, such a ban seems like labelling the New Testament as sexist because Jesus Christ only appointed men to his ministry and racist because the men were all (presumably) Jews. Even in 1996 when Trocadero was bidding for the rights of Enid Blyton's books, the author was denounced for having a bad influence on children. (A bad influence when one considers the drug culture, paedophiles, child abuse and so on!)

Authors reflect the customs and prejudices of their times. The percipient few see that these prejudices can be altered, and set out to do so – but practically never in a text book or children's story. Enid Blyton reflected the world as she saw it when she wrote her books. They do have the virtue of encouraging children to read.

If you want to achieve success in the text book field, however, you should know the outlook of committees who can influence your sales. It is also very important to know in detail the syllabus of any particular exam to which your book is geared. I once took over a class at Christmas, when a teacher had gone sick, and found that the students were studying a syllabus that had changed in the previous summer. Had they continued on the same path, they would have ended up in the following year knowing hardly anything of relevance to the exam they were taking. So always check the syllabus for this year and, if possible, the next four or five. If your book is good, you will be asked to do another edition later. Whether your readers are university or primary students, aim to write simply, mixing your expertise with affection.

A publisher might tell you that an examiner or other person is also writing a book on the same subject and would like to collaborate with you. You may be afraid to disagree lest you prejudice your chance of publication. Be careful. The examiner may be marvellous at spotting mistakes in students' outpourings, no good at creating work of his own. Agree to collaborate only if you can make some sensible arrangement about the ground each covers with equal credit by joint names on the cover. If you refuse, and the publisher does not want your work published under your name, go elsewhere.

Which brings up the subject of duplication. Should you photocopy your book synopsis and sample chapters and send them to more than one publisher? In the case of articles for magazines, newspapers or other journals, the rule is rigid: one piece for one publisher. If an editor likes an article you have done elsewhere and asks you write on the same subject, this is a different kettle of fish. Write it in a different way.

But when one hears how long some book publishers take to report on a few chapters and that some do not even bother to return the manuscript even when an SAE is enclosed, one understands the temptation of new writers to shorten the waiting time for a reply. A newcomer might chance sending duplicate manuscripts to say three publishers, when conscience allows. If by some extraordinary coincidence all of them actually want to publish, take the best offer. You're obviously too good to hang about. The alternative to duplication might be to wait six months or even longer and then get an apology for the late reply to your submission owing to 'moving offices'. The reader's report that "this work is excellent but we have unfortunately arranged for another to be published on the same subject", is no consolation. It merely rubs salt into the wound.

Confessions

You may never have felt the need to confess your sins because you don't regard them as such or, happily, their memory has gone. You have never used the anonymity of the confessional in any language, neither in minor chapels nor major cathedrals, as a way of unloading your guilt; never visited a sympathetic 'shrink', never written to or phoned an 'agony' column to help you out with any problems whatever.

You are therefore probably unaware of the big market that exists for the publication of 'confessions'. Ignore the somewhat lurid pages that go under this title. . . (one can buy/sell anything at a price). Concentrate instead on how to earn an honourable penny or two by writing for readers who are looking for entertainment, interest and, usually, romance.

The market for confessions covers both articles and stories: the articles are usually known as think pieces and, like the stories, are always written in the first person: I did this; I believed, I see now. . . etc. This kind of 'Think' piece usually comes from experts. It covers all kinds of subjects for all types of papers and magazines. You are unlikely to find a market writing think pieces of this kind unless you have some particular specialism, can write with extraordinary passion on a topic of universal interest, or are well known for some special activity.

An example of 'confessions' which offered both a unique and universal appeal were two groups of features, one on Guilt and one on Confessions, which by an apparently odd coincidence, appeared in The *Sunday Telegraph* and *The Observer* in the very same week.

The *Sunday Telegraph* featured true confessions from seven brave and famous people about incidents in their past which still caused them embarrassment. *The Observer* dealt with the subject of Guilt saying that only saints and psychiatrists felt immune. Fourteen famous and not so famous writers contributed their personal reflections on themes such as Abortion, Aids, Children, Crime, Divorce, Infidelity, Jobs, Money, Parents, Religion and so on.

In both magazines there was not one article on these related topics of Guilt and Confession which did not make fascinating reading. And the reason is not hard to find. Readers wonder what they would do in the same circumstances. They identify with the dilemma: 'There, but for the grace of God, go I'. Better still, the authors were generally famous, with a sprinkling of the lesser known, doubtless to show that we are all brothers (or sisters) under the skin.

A more common outlet for confessions used to be in the 'true story' type of magazine. This market is now dwindling unless you can make a TV documentary out of the story or target it to a page of the dailies. They are now filling the True Confessions gap with health, romance and sex related 'confessions'. Women's magazines also highlight firsthand experiences which have a message for their readers.

Because beginners usually have a 'fresher' outlook, their chance of publication in the confessions market is as good as that of the seasoned veteran. Writing requirements are: first person narrative ('I did this or I did that'), target audience generally between 20 and 45+ years for the dailies (much younger for the magazines); a love interest; and characters and problems with which readers can identify.

To break into the market, first consider the age and preferences of your audience. Advertisements in the magazines give you good clues. So do the answers to readers' questions. What kind of jobs do they have? How much do they earn? Where do they live? When you have answered these questions, check on the style of the magazine. Is it breezy, chatty or serious? Are there any subjects which are not welcome? Is sex lightly touched upon, or heavily emphasised? Do the seasons of the year affect the type of story published?

From your perusal of the magazines, you will see that simple and sincere writing about marital or moral problems offers the best chance of publication and of getting a little fame and fortune. Simple and sincere writing is not as easy as it sounds. You need imagination and sympathy to portray realistic characters and write credible dialogue. British stories (they can be more lurid in the US) generally appeal to and are written by younger women, though a man occasionally 'confesses'. Older narrators lessen the chance of publication. A grandmother may be allowed to hover in the background.

Plots tend to be of two types. The first can be summed up as sin, suffer and repent. The heroine commits or allows something she feels wrong to be done (a one-night stand with a person not her husband; an abortion; an anonymous letter, etc.), suffers for it, repents and becomes a reformed character with everything working out to the almost happy ending (almost. . . because guilt often lingers on).

The second type of true story is the 'come to realise' one. The heroine 'comes to realise' a defect in her character which is causing grief to her husband/mother/children; spoiling her chance of a happy marriage, or unhappiness for her boss/colleagues, employees. Alternatively, she 'comes to realise' the hidden goodness in some character she has previously ignored/despised. (He invariably turns out to be rich as well.) Thereafter, all is sweet reason and light. Happiness is restored. This type of story alters to allow for changing social attitudes so that the problems of second wives/husbands relating to each other and stepchildren are now much more frequent.

Pay for true stories, except in the dailies or for prestigious 'confessors', is not among the highest, but payment is usually made earlier than the usual six weeks, sometimes longer after publication, often the case with other outpourings.

Many apparently quite ordinary young women with small families make themselves a good income from specialising in 'confessions'. If you can write simple English (get yourself a dictionary), create sympathetic characters and credible dialogue and are prepared to study what the published writers are producing, you can do the same, or better.

The 'confession' type of story offers an outlet for magazine fiction and in the case of health related subjects can be of great help to other readers suffering similar problems. Experience gained in this market will also help you enter the larger field of women's magazine and romantic novels, where the sky is, very nearly, the limit.

The Trade Press

In the days when I was scratching a living from writing about anything, from tidying up the children's bedrooms (published as Unconsidered Trifles in *The Guardian*), to a not entirely dissimilar topic: the dustbins of Cologne (published in *Municipal Engineering Journal*), I was rung up by the editor of a trade magazine.

Staff writers and famous journalists are used to being approached by editors asking in dulcet tones, 'Can you do me 1,000 words on Pensions or. . . How to Make a Million, or Bringing up a Brighter Baby'. . . etc. For me, a call by an editor actually asking me to write something for his magazine was, at that time, almost akin to a vision on the road to Damascus.

True, I had recently produced my great epic The Packaging of Rindless Pigs, about that most thrilling of topics, the breakfast bacon. And I had also done a piece on Danger, Woman at Work, based on a typical morning when I was bashing out something on the typewriter (published in *Punch* as Beggar My Neighbour) and simultaneously making toys for about five of my own children, and even more, it seemed, of the neighbours'.

The editor of the trade magazine, an architects' journal, said he had seen some of my published work and thought I would be the person for the job he had in mind: to describe, in 3,000 words, the advantages and disadvantages of moving a whole factory and many of its work people from London to a new location. The amount he offered for this job seemed like a small fortune compared with the amounts I got from writing pieces for women in the provincial press.

Probably his original contributor had failed him at the last minute, he had a deadline to meet, by luck had just spotted the first and only contribution I had made to a technical magazine, and thought I might fill the breach. But mine not to reason why – mine just to do and die, though I hoped it wouldn't come to that. I did not even stop to think whether I could manage the job. At the rate offered, who couldn't?

That experience taught me that there was a whole new writing world I had never much thought about, namely producing material for trade, technical and professional magazines. Not all pay highly. Some indeed can hardly balance their budgets and veer between the next issue being the most marvellous ever or sending the publisher into bankruptcy.

The trade press can be subdivided into several groups. There are the journals produced mainly for members of a particular profession. Thus we have *Accountancy* and *Accountancy Age, The Lawyer, The Banker, The Times Educational Supplement,* and *Pensions World.*

In their pages, new trends, legislation or techniques are described which might affect the recruitment, status, training or salary of readers. The advertisements feature appointments, services and products likely to be of interest to them, and there are sometimes interviews with leading figures in the profession such as the Banking or Insurance Ombudsman, or the relevant Minister in Parliament. Some, like *Medeconomics* (Haymarket

Press), targeted at (mainly) GPs, are distributed free, because they include enough advertisements to cover their costs and make a profit.

Then there are technical journals dealing with new developments in a particular industry such as oil, gold, coal, chemicals, cars, computers. They appeal to different groups, ranging from the most technically sophisticated chemical engineer to a youngster interested only in computer games, or his parents wanting to find out the best car or yacht currently on the market.

A growing market is the leisure industry with *Tennis World*, and similar magazines catering for specialised hobbies and leisure pursuits such as car maintenance, angling, caravan holidays, music, theatre.

There are also the hybrids in the form of booklets published by different associations and distributed free to target groups who it is hoped will buy the products or services of the publishing group. The booklets focus on a particular area of interest such as Pensions, Retirement or Saving for Children and a well known journalist is usually asked to write the contents. However if you have a bee in your bonnet, say about the environment or ethical investment, you can be sure that there is an organisation around to promote your cause, and who may be glad of your talent and enthusiasm to write the contents of its magazine, brochure or newsletter. Look around for an organisation that propagates your views and offer your services.

The house magazines subsidised by an industry, company or association are similar but are usually produced 'in house', that is, by the company or organisation concerned. They are like information sheets telling staff of promotions or personnel changes and technical developments within the company.

Most of these publications provide opportunities for the person who aims to make money from writing. The emphasis is on accurate, up-to-date, expert information. Some pay extremely well, and because they often need longer articles than you could get published elsewhere, the total sum earned from your effort will be that much greater. Further, though you cannot hope to compete on a regular basis with the top names in the national press, you can often carve out a regular and profitable niche for yourself in the trade and professional press.

The exception is the house magazine where the opportunity for outsiders to earn anything is limited. There is nothing however to stop you writing to companies to ask whether they would like you to produce a brochure on some product or service for which they want publicity. The pay for writing anything akin to publicity is much higher than for more objective press articles. As a beginner you submit work to a newspaper or magazine, at 'the usual rates'. For freelance work which publicises a product or a service, you should expect and get much more. So if you have any kind of expertise, belong to a trade or profession, and cannot aspire to a book, have a go at writing for the trade press.

Don't patronise. Your readers may be far more intelligent than you are yourself though, for the moment, they just don't know as much about the subject as you do. If something is 'too complicated to discuss here' then do not discuss it here. Write only about what you know, for the person who doesn't but could, if you simply passed the knowledge on.

Ghost Writing

You have doubtless never seen a ghost. You almost certainly have read one. Almost all those wonderful articles and books on how this or that star made it to the top; their history portrayed in glorious Technicolor on the bookstalls, and in more muted jackets that you see in the public libraries: very many of these are lives as told to the ghost.

The ghost in this case is the writer of the 'life'. He or she interviews the celebrity, and with the help of background information, notes and interviews, sometimes taped, writes the life story or that part of it most interest to the public. Sometimes ghost writers get their names on the front covers with their celebrities; sometimes they have to remain anonymous, exchanging fame for a fortune that is peanuts compared with that of their live counterparts.

But there are often peaks and troughs in literary earnings. Ghosted interviews, books and articles can fill out the troughs. They sharpen up your writing skills, and can be a useful line of activity in which to earn money when other work is not so easily obtainable.

Choose interesting personages who have achieved some distinction or notoriety for your 'ghosting'. If you have contacts known for some activity, or unique experiences, but who are too busy, modest or discreet to write their own life stories, there could be an opening for you. Or you may be a 'fan' of some actor, actress or sportsperson, with understanding and knowledge of their lives, and an enthusiasm for all that they do.

In either case, you need to find a market before you 'write them up'. Compared with other writing activity, this is the easiest part. First make the suggestion to the most likely editor: fashion, politics, economics, or a 'women's' column. Having roused his interest and agreement, and shown that you are the person to do this job, ask the celebrity for an interview. They will almost invariably agree.

Even if the style of your resultant copy is not quite what the editor wanted, he or his subs will soon bring it up to the required standard. Ask to see proofs so you can ensure that nothing goes in which is against the spirit of the piece. Your name may not appear at all. The column may be headed 'X or Y speaks on. . .' You are merely the 'ghost', though this is not always the case. Sometimes you, too, will get a by-line.

The distinction between contract writing, when you research and write for a publication under contract, and ghost writing is that under the latter, you write to someone else's material under a name not your own. Many celebrities are incapable of writing readable feature articles, and there is no reason why a man who has a talent for scoring goals or winning boxing championships should be expected also to have writing skills. Even literate celebrities such as those with one or more books to their credit may be too busy or too shy to publicise themselves in a magazine or newspaper. They may also be unable to write in the style of the particular newspaper or magazine, and produce pages of waffle instead of keeping to their brief of, for example, 'The people who helped me achieve success', or 'Tips I learnt on my way up'.

Even when the celebrity has the necessary writing skill, he may not be able to undertake a contractual series. This is where the ghost creeps in. He or she has to produce words that sound as if they came from the celebrity. Ghost writing about sportspeople is easier than for comedians, who in real life may be more thoughtful and intelligent than they appear on screen, or when doing their act.

Insert a few of their jokes into your article. This will not only make it more readable, it will also help to give the 'flavour' of the comedian about whom you are writing. Use a tape recorder for interviews. There are two reasons for this. One is that people often speak more naturally, after perhaps a bout of initial inhibition, than they would do to a shorthand writer. Dialogue adds colour to your writing and makes it come alive. The transcript is also useful to recall any dates or episodes that were mentioned (though it is wise to check these). To avoid libel, if nothing else, let your celebrity view your efforts before they are printed.

Ghost writers can also be active in books. The same technique applies as in writing an interview. First get your man or woman to agree, though if you are known to move in certain circles where notables mingle, you may be approached by a publisher first, with a suggestion that you write up this or that life.

Fees will be discussed then. The celebrities may have their own ideas about what their ghostly lives are worth. Unless you are a good negotiator, you will invariably come off second best. But having successfully completed one project, you will have no difficulty in getting another with higher rewards even for a lesser 'life'. Fees are negotiated independently of the royalty system. They usually depend on the relative wealth or poverty of the client you are ghosting for, the difficulty of handling the material, the time scale, and the expertise and ability of the author. The usual arrangement is a fixed fee, and no royalty arrangement as with contract publishing.

If ghost writing appeals to you, and you are not bothered by having to remain anonymous, try one of the companies offering production services in *Yellow Pages, The Writer's Handbook* or the *Writers' and Artists' Year Book*. They have had clients as varied as a Muslim in Pakistan who provided a corneal graft for a Hindu and topics as different as child abuse in a children's home and a true wartime story in the Channel Islands. Alternatively, you can try an agent if one will take you on. But they are hard to find and, if found, will want their reward too.

Poetry

Titles like *Poetry, Bloody Poetry* which I saw being read on a commuter train are somewhat different from those of my youth, but there has been a large increase in poetry book sales in the past five years. Publishers are jumping on to the bandwagon of an increased awareness of this branch of literature.

But can a newcomer gain much by writing poetry? Alas, the answer, in terms of financial reward at least, must be NO. Generally speaking, it is not the newcomers but the established names who are gaining from renewed attention.

Genius is one tenth inspiration, nine tenths perspiration, but a new poet often needs medication as well. Life is hard, at least in terms of payment for work done. Poets link sounds and phrases to make an audience think and feel. That is their aim and often their only reward.

Like artists, they try to communicate a vision sometimes only they can see, and like artists, they have to wait perhaps in vain for their worth to be recognised or understood. Sometimes, however, like Stevie Smith, they get a double bonus. Her *Novel on Yellow Paper* came out in 1938, but as an accomplished reader of her own verse, she earned another generation of admirers three decades later.

Some help to aspiring writers can come from the work of other poets. Look at the fairly modern ones like Sylvia Plath, the Poet Laureate Ted Hughes, Philip Larkin and John Betjeman, whose subjects and style are so recognisable.

W. H. Auden produces striking syllables and sounds, and has written at least two poems particularly relevant to writers. In *The Novelist,* he contrasts the poet who amazes us "like a thunderstorm", with the novelist who has to be all things to all men; who, in order to write about a subject, has to feel it, be it, live it.

Somewhat similar are Auden's sonnets on *The Composer* and *Edward Lear.* But his work is uneven and, at times, almost inscrutable. When I asked him to 'translate' a couple of lines in his poem, *Streams,* he replied with even more Delphic utterance "1. The God of mortal Doting, is, as you guessed, Eros. The vision and its properties are meant to be a kind of modernised Petrachian *Triofo d'Amore.* 2. He thanks all the people in the dream, the X and Y to whom he promises a passion undying, are, neither of them, presumably, the Dreamer himself (the 'I' of the poem...)".

Yet this same poet wrote *Musee des Beaux Arts:* a thought provoking piece on one of Auden's favourite subjects: suffering. He declares the great masters were never wrong on this theme, and describes the painting of Icarus by Breughel. Icarus, the son of Daedalus in Greek mythology, flies with his father from Crete. The sun melts the wax which fastens his wings to his ankle. He falls into the sea and is drowned.

Breughel's painting shows that in spite of this terrible, indeed extraordinary, happening of a man falling from the sky into the sea, life elsewhere, and even in the vicinity, proceeds on its normal course. And that, says Auden, is what epitomises suffering: somebody experiencing pain or tragedy while the rest of the world continues its normal business, uncaring ('. . . how it takes place? While someone else is eating or opening a window or just walking dully along?') .

The American Robert Frost has a way of making you think differently about quite everyday subjects. Read *Mending Wall.* It shows how platitudes like, 'Good fences make good neighbours' can boomerang. Are fences, Frost asks, for walling in or walling out?

Pit your own work against these craftsmen, but not too harshly. If you have written poems without a single effort being published, try putting them together and submitting them as a collection. Books still sell well, and you might have better luck than with one or two poems. When trying a magazine, however, send only a single submission.

Your best chances of publication are in literary, upmarket journals. These include *Agenda, Ambit, London Magazine, New Statesman, The Spectator, Orbis* and *The Times Literary Supplement. Poetry Review* is distributed to institutions, libraries and schools. Don't expect much in the way of payment except from newspapers and all but the biggest magazines. It is usually nominal. Some publications and the small presses have barely enough resources to pay for their printing and postage costs.

Poetry Nottingham (39 Cavendish Road, Long Eaton, Nottingham NG10 4HY) make no payment, but if they publish your poem (not more than 30 lines), they send you a complimentary copy of the magazine with your entry. This can be a big boost. When you have not previously had any verse in print, seeing your work in a magazine gives you the encouragement and confidence to try again with perhaps greater rewards next time.

By contrast with the comparatively small number of markets for poetry, there are numerous competitions and awards for poets, regionally and nationally. These are well worth entering. All the Arts Councils offer them. Festival and other prizes are listed under the Poetry section in the Guide to Literary Prizes and Awards from the Book Trust. Check also with your local library or newspaper for possible competitions, festivals and one-off events in your locality. They are not always advertised nationally.

Entries for poetry prizes may have to be submitted by publishers, but individual entries are usually accepted by organisers of literary festivals, such as the Aldeburgh Poetry Festival, sponsored by Waterstone and the Aldeburgh Bookshop. For an updated directory of competitions and awards contact The Poetry Society (0171 240 4810), membership £24 annually. The National Poetry Competition is a major national event with prizes worth £4,000 (lst), £1,000 (2nd), £500 (3rd) and a special category for poems of 40–100 lines (£1,000). Closing date is 30 October. Rules and entry form from the Competition Organiser, The Poetry Society, 22 Betterton Street, London WC2H 9BU.

Literary societies and Arts associations provide grants and bursaries for aspiring poets. Among them is The Arvon Foundation. With this help, it runs four and a half day residential writing courses at a subsidised rate. The foundation has three centres in West Yorkshire, Devon and Inverness. It organises workshops for published and unpublished writers in all genres and runs an international biennial competition for previously unpublished poems written in English (first prize is £5,000; another £5,000 in cash prizes). Details from the Arvon Foundation, Kilnhurst, Kilnhurst Road, Todmorden, Lancs. A new writing course has also started for teachers, who may fear they are losing their creativity after marking so much of their students' work.

Do not get too downhearted if you get no financial reward from your solitary outpourings. Press on.

How-To-Do-It

You cannot have reached the age you have without learning something. You may not even realise that you possess talents and skills which other people would like to acquire. But do you realise that you can, for example, make jam, chutney, an apple tart, strawberry flan, or cook pork with gooseberry sauce? Perhaps you fish, sail, knit, sew, embroider, or crochet? Are you a dab hand with the camera, an expert driver, motor mechanic, plumber, carpenter, electrician? An architect, doctor, solicitor? Do you know of wonderful places for camping, skiing, water sports, walking, in the UK or abroad? There are readers everywhere who want to read of your activities, hobbies and skills.

Such leisure or full time pursuits can be put to another use: earning you a secondary or, in some cases, a primary income. There is only one exception: sport. Nobody wants advice from a tennis player who came fourth in the local club handicap, or from a footballer in the lowest division of the League.

Articles or books on any aspect of sport sell only from athletes, golfers or swimmers; tennis, football, hockey, baseball or squash players who have made it to the top. You may be able to ghost their books. . . that is a different story. But except for sport, you can ignore Shaw's dictum: He who can, does; he who cannot, teaches. For you it is doing and teaching through writing.

To move into this profitable 'how-to-do-it' field, ask yourself the following questions: would somebody else find my knowledge useful; do I know of any short cuts or tips in my work? If your answer is yes, a never ending source of income opens up before you.

It is not only in the non fiction field that your work can earn you money by telling others how to do what you can do. Fiction, too, needs realism. You have only to think of the racing novels of Dick Francis. A National Hunt jockey in 1946, he became Champion Jockey in 1953–4 and his first book was published in 1962. He has written a best selling one every year since, with wife Mary doing much of the research.

Or consider the runaway success of *Doctor in the House* by Richard Gordon based partly on his own experience. Another example of background experience helping to produce a book with the stamp of authenticity are the Rumpole books written by John Mortimer and visualised for many non readers in a TV series.

Henry Cecil, in his memoirs *Just Within the Law*, tells how his own success came about. He found that when he went into the Army, fellow officers liked the stories he invented about the law. When he sailed for the Middle East, the voyage took two months. Cecil used the evenings telling tales to the troops as a form of entertainment. The stories were typed out in the Middle East and sent to Macmillan in the UK for publication. Cecil's first wife Lettice and Cecil himself, after he returned home, tried several more publishers after his manuscript was returned. No luck. He felt that however much he wrote, he could improve his style only marginally, so if no one intended to publish his work, he would write no more.

How-To-Do-It

Then a lucky break intervened. His father, who collected stamps as a hobby, had a stamp collector friend with a daughter. The daughter's friend had a 12 year old sister, called Naomi, with whom Cecil used to correspond until she was grown up. Naomi eventually went to the US, joining the American branch of the literary agents Curtis Brown. Coming to England for a holiday, she mentioned Juliet O'Hea who worked in the English office of the same agents. Cecil asked her to get him an introduction, which she did. Juliet suggested substituting two stories in Cecil's unpublished manuscript, *Full Circle,* sent the altered version round to several publishers, and eventually succeeded with Chapman & Hall. It was the *seventeenth* time the manuscript had gone out.

Cecil tells this story so that authors should not despair if their first book is rejected. He also warns them not to expect too much if it gets published. When his own came out, he rushed round bookstalls everywhere looking for it, and couldn't find a single copy. Luck was kind to Henry Cecil, eventually. Since that time he has written 33 books and many radio plays, some original, others based on his books. But he would never have made it as an author if he had not written the book. And all he did was to tell stories arising out of his background knowledge.

Sir David Napley, who has been president of London (Criminal Courts) Solicitors' Association, similarly used his work expertise in his writing, while Edgar Lustgarten is another lawyer who relied on a legal background to bring famous legal cases to life for his readers. Travellers too, who assault mountains, sail the seven seas, struggle through snowy wastes or dried up deserts, often tell marvellous tales of how they did or – equally readable – didn't achieve their aim.

So analyse what you can do, that others can't, then write

about it. Unless you are absolutely bursting to do a book, in which case nothing will stop you, begin with small projects, 'fillers' perhaps that fill a column in magazines. Do not ignore radio. Many people find it easier to hear how to do a thing than read about it, especially if the speaker is easy to follow. Gardening programmes, woodworking, looking after your car, your house, all fill occasional radio slots. As always, study the market. Get yourself on mailing lists, trade associations. When writing, as when speaking, make the piece relevant to your audience. Topicality is only of minor interest here.

Give materials needed, if any, and some idea of the costs and rewards of the labour. Excellent examples of 'how-to-do-it' are the knitting patterns and cookery menus in many of the women's magazines and newspapers. The latter list the ingredients and amounts needed for the recipe, their cost, preparation, cooking time and oven temperature. They are often accompanied by such attractive illustrations of the finished product and read so easily that even the most inexpert cook, such as me, is tempted to 'have a go'. And that is exactly the reaction you will get from your reader if you show your expertise in the simplest way you can.

Develop a Specialism

You may be lucky or talented enough to get an article accepted occasionally but how do you increase this writing income? The answer is don't generalise, specialise. Manuscripts on general subjects may be sometimes easier to place, but if you develop a specialism, you learn more, earn more and become better known.

Writing on special subjects like law, taxation, medicine, accountancy and finance are not the same as 'how-to-do-it' articles. Specialist articles inform; the 'how-to-do-it' kind tell you how to perform a job or a craft or acquire a skill. Specialist medical articles therefore inform you about health, illness, the human body. They don't say how you too can become a practitioner.

Similarly the works of a specialist legal writer are not 'how to. . .' articles, though they may (rarely) tell you how to get the best from your solicitor. They are informative about certain aspects of the law, often illustrated by amusing or unusual anecdotes.

Obviously some specialisms cannot be easily acquired. The doctor cannot become a lawyer overnight, or vice versa, though both can soon become politicians. The qualifications which enable you to practise certain professions take three to five years, sometimes longer. Even teaching, which many people think they can do until they enter some of the schoolrooms of today, needs a three to four year qualifying period and a probationary year after that. (Evening class teaching is somewhat different, relying on practical skills and different exams or experience.)

Nevertheless it is possible by reading, practice, attending seminars, and so on, to acquire a fund of learning about a particular topic. The more you write and research on that topic, the more you learn about it, and the more often you will be asked by editors to write on some aspect of it.

As a way of explaining and encouraging you in the art of the specialism, I give here a resumé of how I entered the specialist field of financial journalism. Over the years I had written many pieces about family topics. Editors often made their acceptances with a little note, 'like to see more work, without prejudice', but only a few of them actually telephoned or wrote to commission further pieces.

Then one day I saw a copy of a new magazine, called *What Investment*. Inside was a series on British financial institutions with a highly readable article on the Stock Exchange, written in her inimitably authoritative yet simple style by Diana Wright, then a prolific freelance writer who later became Personal Finance Editor of *The Sunday Times*.

I had an Oxford University qualification in economics and had been teaching it for some years, but never wrote any articles on the subject, mainly because there seemed so many experts around already. However, needing some cash, I approached the editor of *What Investment* with an idea.

This approach is known as the query. Beginners can try it as a short cut to writing a long article, by sending the idea, title and specimen headings to a prospective editor. A good lead paragraph often helps turn the query into a commission. Enclose a stamped postcard for return with blocks for the editor to tick. This will at least get you a reply. The blocks can have such headings as: Under consideration; hope to publish on. . . other comments, followed by a couple of dotted lines.

I did not use the written query, for it seemed I could sell my idea by phone. This is not an approach to be recommended unless you have a highly topical or unusual idea. The query itself is hardly worthwhile on short articles of 800–1,000 words, for which there might be several markets.

I suggested to the then editor a topic that seemed sufficiently new and unusual (while fitting into the series) to be acceptable: an article on the London Discount Houses. The editor took it and later asked me for more. Having notched that success under my belt, I later approached The *Daily Telegraph* personal finance editor, then Richard Northedge, afterwards promoted to the City pages, with another idea. Kindly, full of good tips, he asked me to send in 750 words, which I did. Whenever I later phoned, I always had two or three ideas as, if one was not liked, another was usually asked for.

Having got a temporary niche in The *Daily Telegraph* at that time, a whole wide world of personal finance articles opened up before me: mortgages, different forms of investment such as gilts, National Savings, Personal Equity Plans, and so on, which I could place in many different magazines.

Changes in legislation cause the topic of personal finance to be constantly changing. I was lucky enough to enter this field during a bull market. But even during a recession, the opportunity for specialist writing on personal finance continues, because new products and services are always coming to the market.

I eventually got a regular outlet and no longer sought freelance work. It comes to me. This personal experience shows that developing a specialism can be done. To be successful, follow these tips:

- do not enter a field where qualifications acquired over many years are necessary

- have or get some basic knowledge of the subject in which you are interested and in which you hope to specialise BUT

- make sure that there is a big market for you in that area

- check the adverts as a clue to that market

- get on to public relations consultancies, trade organisations and others who will send you press releases and news of developments in your special field

- develop your basic knowledge by reading and research

Well known novelists occasionally write under different names because they are producing something different or special from their usual format. What is good for them is also good for you. Develop a specialism along with any other writing you do, and you may well find the first overtakes and is more rewarding than the latter.

Self Help

Even for journalists who write for a living, the idea of producing a book often seems too lengthy and tortuous a path to pursue. For those who have never published anything at all, the effort is even harder. Don't be dismayed, A journey of a thousand miles begins with a single step. For writers, the first step is the first word and self publishing can be the first word. Avoid answering advertisements ('vanity publishing') asking for new authors. Any enquiry usually brings the response that your work can be published if you share the publishing costs. Succumb to the temptation and the 'share' will be very heavy and you will have to store and sell every copy of your book.

There are occasions, however, when publishing your own work may be worthwhile. One is when, like J. L. Carr, you already know booksellers and a good printer. Offered for *What Hetty Did* (a novel about an adopted girl's search for her mother) £5,000 advance to include paperback rights, the same figure as three years previously for another book, he decided to do his own publishing. The printer quoted £3,157 for setting, printing and binding the first 1,000 copies, £678 for second and subsequent thousands. J. L. Carr ordered 3,000 books at a cost of £4,587 or £1.52 a copy, with 200 extra for publicity. (It should be noted here that figures are for a decade ago. The advance of technology has made printing, without metal plates, very much cheaper and quicker, though postage has gone up enormously.)

Having reckoned packaging and postage at 30 pence, he gave booksellers a 35% discount on one book (£2.57), 40% discount on orders of five or more (£2.37 each). Unfortunately with packaging and postage costs proving dearer at 43p, 2,200 books had to be sold just to break even. Sales of the whole 3,000 delivered to his door (five weeks after sending in his manuscript to the printer!) would make a mere £320.

He found a freelance rep advertising in *The Bookseller*, paid him 10% on sales and the whole issue was sold within seven weeks. . . a great success, you may think. Yet for all that work and expertise, the return was a few hundred pounds. Fortunately it was not the end of the story. The BBC bought the script for the *Book at Bedtime* slot at £7.95 a minute (January 1989) and J. L. Carr ordered a reprint of another 3,000.

The second instance when it makes sense to write and print your own work is when you want to propagate some cause or theme, even if you make yourself poorer by so doing. Upton Sinclair publicised causes he held dear.

The third time self publishing can work is when you are already known. Edgar Wallace, thrilled at his successful first entry into publishing with 30,000 sales of *Smithy*, tried his luck again with the much rejected *Four Just Men*. He over advertised, lost £1,400 in selling 38,000 copies and sold the remaining book rights to George Newnes for £72.

The most likely chance of success from self publishing, however, is in a business of your own, selling words, not goods. You can work alone or as part of a writing team producing news-letters, brochures, guides or instruction manuals. Offer your services to companies, manufacturers, or public relations firms. Grants or assistance are sometimes available not only for the unemployed but for budding entrepreneurs. Check with the local Department of Employment Job Centre.

Income from writing, in your own business, or another's, depends on motivation, effort and market demand. Without those, profit is likely to be minuscule. Here are three true life examples which emphasise the point.

It has been said that anybody who rides on a bus after the age of 30 is a failure in life. Some time ago when I was just past the age of 30 I was on my way to work in a bus quickly filling to suffocation point. The bus was one of those (now unfortunately almost extinct except in central London) with a conductor as well as a driver.

The conductor stood by the entrance reading a book. He collected no fares, other than those proffered by departing passengers. He made no effort to stop anybody getting on, though the bus was so crammed with bodies that it looked like a Third (or even Fourth) World transport system. And the reason that the conductor was doing absolutely nothing, except ring a bell to start the bus off, was that he was totally immersed in a book. What marvellous author, I wondered, could so hold a man in thrall? Jealous of such literary talent, I tried, head up and down, to see its title.

In vain. When the journey ended, and passengers had dug themselves out of the mêlée, I gave the conductor his uncollected fare, and asked to see the book. For the first time on the whole journey, he came alive. His eyes glowed as he extolled its virtues. The title? I couldn't believe it and you'll never guess: *Self Help* by Samuel Smiles (a case of theory without practice?).

The second tale concerns an editor, Richard Bunning. A

young computer consultant, he saw an opening for a magazine different from those containing adverts for computers and from agencies who, if successful in placing staff, earn large fees. In his back bedroom, Richard began the magazine, *Freelance Informer*. Illustrated, lively, full of a kind of clean undergraduate humour, peppered with job experiences here and abroad and with revenue from adverts, it went out on subscription and was an almost immediate hit.

His workload was tremendous but four years after *Freelance Informer* started, Reed Publishing made an offer which Richard could not, as the saying goes, refuse, though he remained on for some time as editor. After he left, the first page of the magazine continued to bear the inscription: Founded by Richard Bunning.

Lastly, there is William Harrison of Worcester, a college lecturer who, dissatisfied with the lack of books on accountancy for bankers, decided to write his own. He knew nothing of printers' costs, but his accountancy knowledge saved him from pitfalls. The book was printed and did extremely well. He spent two days weekly in London talking to booksellers such as Foyle's and WH Smith ('both very helpful' he recollects) and four years later gave up teaching, which he much enjoyed, as the publishing escalated.

He has brought out 14 titles, and successful home study courses, and tells me he has been approached many times with takeover bids for his Northwick Publishing company,

Unless you want to remain an unpublished novelist reading *Self Help* by Samuel Smiles, the moral seems to be that NOW is the time to get started and do your own thing.

Writing Speeches

Speeches that are given at seminars and conferences usually have to be written before they are spoken. Even when the speaker gives the impression of ad libbing or speaking off the cuff, he (or she) may have well prepared the piece from a written synopsis.

For some people, however, there is a barrier between their thoughts and putting them down in any readable form. If this is your situation, and you are called upon to make a speech longer than a few happy words at some domestic ceremony, first jot down a few headings. Speak into a cassette, expanding on those headings. When you finish, transcribe your speech to paper.

At meetings of the more cosy kind, such as a cookery talk at the local library or women's institute, you will not be asked to give the text of your speech, but it often helps you to give a better performance. You will be asked back again, with hopefully a higher fee, or your expenses covered.

Even if you are well known in your own field, a transcript will be required of you for any fairly high powered conferences. People often pay several hundred pounds to attend such conferences, and usually get a press pack containing the text of the lectures or speeches made at the meeting.

30 Ways To Make Money – IN WRITING

Roger Caroll, a past Personal Finance editor for The *Sunday Telegraph*, has written speeches for many of the top 'brass' of the political parties, including Prime Ministers. His columns are most readable, even on what to the layman are often complex subjects. They also have those rare qualities in financial journalism, a touch of humour and grace.

He gives the following suggestions for anybody wishing to make or write a speech. Unless you are a talented ad libber, a professional entertainer, or speaking at a domestic celebration, compose and preferably write your speech before you attempt to deliver it.

He also stresses that, excluding poetry, rhythm is far more important in speaking than writing. Speech writing should therefore allow for pauses, emphasis, staccato. A good exercise which shows how important rhythm is to the spoken word is to take any line of poetry and alter one of the words, or transpose them so that they are in a different order. The first line to come to my mind begins that unforgettable piece in *Hamlet* which sums up so pithily the dilemma facing a person choosing whether to live or die.

The line is "To be, or not to be, that is the question. . ." Change it round to "To exist, or not to exist, that is the question". The sense is the same but do those words have the same ring as the original? In German, the contrast is even greater.

Do this exercise of alteration (or transposition) for any other line of poetry to see how important is its rhythm. The same holds true for a speech. Give it a beat, if only at the end of a line.

Another piece of advice for those who want to write speeches as a way of increasing or creating interest (and income) is to

Writing Speeches

use antithesis. For those who have long forgotten school grammar, antithesis is a figure of speech showing opposites or contrasts. Thus we can say (as most economists do), 'On the one hand, this, on the other hand, that'. . . or ' Those who live by the sword, must die by the sword' . . . or ' If they have no bread, let them eat cake. . .' and so on.

To keep an audience awake, especially at company meetings, throw in a few antitheses. They are good, too, for political meetings. Party X said they would increase this. . . and what have they done? 'Decreased it. . .'

The third element in good speech writing is the 'list', or set of three references. Thus. . . 'we will do this, and this, and that.' Or 'the opposing party has not kept any of its promises. It has failed to do this. It has failed to do this, and it has failed to do the other'. Roger Caroll says that two in a list do not have the power and emphasis of three, while four are too many.

It sometimes pays to lighten the 'dough' of a speech with the yeast of humour. Put in some relevant joke at the beginning to attract and hold the attention of your listeners. If you do not get them early, they will fiddle about in their seats, read the chairman's report or the press pack, or watch other people in the audience. So use the beginning, middle and end for a bit of humour. Not too much. . . the meeting is probably a serious one, particularly if it concerns finance, and flippancy or anything akin to it will ensure you are not asked again.

Try for a good conclusion. The O. Henry type of short story with a twist at the end is no good for modern articles, where if the editor has to cut he snips off your last paragraph which cost you so much time and effort. In speeches that does not happen; the final paragraph is the one to earn the most applause.

People often speak at meetings or seminars to publicise

their companies, products and services. They do not need or require payment. The publicity gained is reward enough. You are in a different position. Look up adverts giving details of forthcoming events and meetings. Write to the organisers, saying you can write on a subject relevant to the organisation's aims and objectives.

Write also to people who are in the limelight with offers to create their speeches for them. Give details of your background and experience. When a guest speaker is taken ill or unable to attend, you could be asked at very short notice to attend. Fees for speeches vary from expenses only at parish meetings and clubs to over £1,000 for a 30 minute talk that will, however, take much longer to prepare. Such fees are usually only paid to notable personalities, so it is worthwhile cultivating them by the brilliance of your pen. But if you have a clear voice, confidence, some good contacts or the ability to make them, speech writing can give a significant boost to your income.

The Story Of Your Life

"... I sometimes think only autobiography is literature."
(Virginia Woolf)

The story of a person's life, written by that person, often produces the most fascinating read. When other books fail to interest or inspire, the autobiography can still transport a reader into new worlds. Such works are generally written by people who are or have been in the public eye: such as actors, sportspeople or politicians.

But humble lives can be of equal interest, revealing a piece of social and economic history. Your autobiography may not immediately bring you in an income, but will be treated as riches by your family. It is a key to their past.

To show you that there is something of interest in your life story, here is the tale of two streets. To an outsider both of them appear to be like hundreds of others in their respective neighbourhoods. The first, now swept away by slum clearance, was the one in which I grew up: a little group of terraced houses in London's East End.

As kids we played there, when we came home from our schools in Bethnal Green, Hoxton, Spitalfields or Whitechapel. Shoved off by one neighbour for fear we should break a window, we would move to another section and if a window was broken by a ball, the householder would repair it herself and come charging along to our mothers for a bit of compensation (and be lucky if she could get it).

A few doors away from us lived a young widow with a 13 year old daughter. Her happy go lucky appearance told nobody she was so heavily into debt she was about to lose her home with only the workhouse to turn to. When her daughter arrived home from school one day, she found her mother dead, hanging from the stairs.

Mrs. X farther up the road had a large family, but also committed suicide. She chose drowning as her exit from life, by throwing herself into the lake in Victoria Park. An unsuccessful builder in the street staged a more elaborate death by hanging from scaffolding in Bethnal Green Road. Sadder still was the suicide of the distraught father who turned on the gas and did away with himself when his beloved daughter died from diphtheria, rife in those days.

As a Jew, his death was of greater horror for the relatives than that of an atheist who chooses the same route. Two more little dramas of that street are worth mentioning: the two young men who built up a wonderful printing business, and then split up, among scenes of such strife, bitterness and family feuding that they made the Capulets and Montagues in Romeo and Juliet seem like sweet talking neighbours.

There were the success stories: the scholarship boy who became a local librarian, and then went off to America's west coast – an incredible journey as we thought. Others of his relatives chose Rhodesia as their destination.

I learnt from them never to tidy up when 'social workers', who could provide homes, grants, or other benefits, came to inspect, but to fill up your rented rooms preferably with a few relatives who were pregnant or ill, easy enough when birth control was in its infancy (so to speak) and TB so prevalent.

The last tale is a personal one. My mother had let for a few days a room to a lodger with an American accent. We were very impressed. One night I was woken up by the sound of somebody creeping up the squeaky stairs to the bedroom where I slept and which had no gas or electricity. My hand shook too much to light the candle and when I tried to scream, the cry died in my throat. My father, who had a tryst with the bottle, came in at that moment, revelling drunk, and woke up everybody with his singing the Rose of Tralee. Life came back to normal. . . or nearly so. Our lodger left next morning for Canada, so he said. Two days later we heard that the old lady who lived in the corner house had been murdered in her bed.

The second street is in suburban Surrey with a lush, sleepy appearance. Yet at least half a dozen houses have known drama that would make newspaper headlines. . . and sometimes did. A policeman there murdered his wife, a devoted mother. Her body was never found. Then there was the family who went on holiday in Devon. The husband took a morning dip accompanied by his young daughter, had a heart attack, and died shortly after he had plunged into the waves. The distraught mother got a little cheer from a son then in South America, telling her that he was getting married, and inviting her out six months later to the wedding.

Preparing to go, she received a cable. It told her that the son and his fiancée, along with two other sweethearts, had gone for a picnic along a river bank. One of the young women, a nurse, fell into the swirling waters. The son rescued her, but drowned in the attempt. The mother went out not to his wedding but to his funeral.

Look around your own street. Every home has a story. That is the attraction of autobiography. In writing the story of one life, you describe many, giving your readers a sense of history, a link with the past. What you will earn from such memoirs is more debatable.

You can read many life stories, from Hans Christian Andersen to H. G. Wells, Edith Wharton and Oscar Wilde, with writers like Rudyard Kipling, Somerset Maugham, millionaires like Paul Getty, and statesmen like Charles de Gaulle in between. (An odd and intriguing one is the Australian *My Brilliant Career* by Miles Franklin.) But all of these, except the last, which took many years to be published, were by well known names.

It is only a chance that your own life story will bring you in an income. Reduce the chance of 'failure' by the following tips:

- break up your life into sections

- highlight the incidents that stand out, rather than writing a sequence of events

- describe turning points in your life – for example: work, marriage, childbirth

- link your story to history: big events in the outside world. Revolutions and natural disasters may have taken place at the same time as a crisis in your own life

- check dates
- create a good title

You may also need a foreword or introduction and a table of contents to let readers and editors know what they're in for. Look up publishers who accept memoirs. Send them a query or your full manuscript and hope for the best.

Humour

To make money by writing humour, you need three main skills. The first is skill with words: far more necessary with humorous writing than any other, except poetry and advertising copy. Almost everything you attempt: jokes, witty articles, amusing books, even sketches or plays – everything except perhaps comic strips (and even here the 'balloon' is almost as important as the pictures), your output almost always begins as words on paper or disk. Even if your work will ultimately be spoken, you must first have, or develop, vocabulary skills. It is unfair and unprofessional to rely on a comedian's mannerisms or an actor's ability to breathe life into leaden prose.

The second skill needed for writing humour is an ability to visualise comic characters, situations, events. A book with an amusing character will often be adapted for a TV series – *Rumpole of the Bailey* by John Mortimer is a case in point. Rumpole is beautifully portrayed by actor Leo McKern, but if John Mortimer had not first created such a convincing character, all Leo McKern's histrionic ability could not have brought him to life for viewers.

Another example of this ability to visualise can be seen in Michael Green's series of books based on the idea of how to be successful without actually trying, as exemplified in *The Art of Coarse Rugby, Office Politics*, etc. Several were adapted into stage plays but began as books visualising humorous situations.

The third necessary skill is an ability to analyse the fragmented market for humour. Jokes may be sold for use in a comic series to a comedian, to radio or TV. Another type of market could be a sophisticated one that enjoys satire and wit rather than slapstick or farce. Articles/stories might go to a magazine for parents who like reading about amusing domestic incidents with which they can identify. Whatever your target audience, you have to make it smile, belly laugh, or chuckle later when the memory of your wit, your comedy, comes back.

Not all jokes or humorous situations appear funny to everyone. As an example, consider the phenomenon of trash TV. *Crime Time,* an all American television show, aimed to bring the underworld of entertainment into the living room. Its creator, Mark Weinberg, former US commodities broker (no connection with any UK person of the same name), called it the "Ed Sullivan show with felons".

He is reputed to have spent $250,000 enticing mobsters to the screen because nobody had tried to do comedy with them. And a lot of murderers, he added, have a great sense of humour. As Dermot Purgavie (brilliant *Mail* commentator of the US scene) succinctly wrote, "Yeah. You could die laughing".

Don't touch anything you do not like. Fun writing should be fun for writer as well as listener and viewer. Try for the humour with an almost universal appeal. Its basis is incongruity, or transposition. This means a change of name, identity, situation. Test for yourself how calling somebody in a group by the wrong name (not with any cruel intent) invariably raises a laugh, especially if two or three around say, 'No, I'm. . ."

In this vein is the tale told of the time in Cairo when the ambassador Miles Lampson became Lord Killearn. Shortly afterwards a visitor lunching with the ambassador and his wife remarked, "It's so nice you're here now and not those Lampsons whom we disliked so much".

Similar examples of the wrong name are a rural area hived off to preserve its natural beauty, and labelled conversation area, instead of conservation area; or an advertisement for a warehouseman who must be 'conscious' (instead of conscientious). Prince Charles, on confessing how he got out of some scrape or other, remarked, "As you see, it pays to know the right people". And it is indeed well to know the right people and the right name, otherwise when you introduce somebody as the King of X, he may modestly reply, no, the King of Y, actually. Or. . . trying to recollect where you have seen a certain person before, because the face is so familiar, you say (hoping they will give you a clue) 'Are you still living in the same place?' and they reply, 'Yes, still at Buckingham Palace'). Mistaken or changed names are also the basis of many humorous plays, such as Oscar Wilde's *The Importance of Being Earnest*.

Topicality helps, especially with a political or satirical edge. During the first stages of the women's lib movement, an 88 year old single woman was asked why in her will she had specified no male pall bearers. "The rotters never took me out while I was alive", she is supposed to have said. "They're not going to take me out when I'm dead."

Formulae are helpful. Among the most useful ones are those like: It was so hot that. . . so cold that. . . so dull that etc.

Another formula involves definitions. You begin with part of a sentence like: 'You all know what a Beetle is...' and then follow it up with your own definition. Similarly with "You know what a think tank, an economist, a banker etc... is'. Then there are **adverbs** to contrast with the rest of a sentence: 'Make the print stronger', the author said **boldly**; 'I like camping', he said **intensely**.

There is also the device of initials. This gives the opportunity for the humorist writer to make jokes at the expense of MPs or MAs by giving the initials different meanings. One rich entrepreneur, unable to write, was told he could sign his name with an X. He signed with two Xs. Asked what the second X was for, he replied "D.Phil.".

With jokes, it helps to try for the style of a well known comedian, and offer them to him/her. Test them on friends. You won't get paid, but you will get a reaction. Humorous novels, of which there seem very few today, can go to general publishers. Articles with satirical humour could find a place in *Private Eye*. Digests take short humorous pieces and pay well for them.

Mother and Baby and *Parents* type magazines always have a niche for humorous articles based on family life such as that of Viscount de L'Isle, who records in *Raise Your Glasses* (collected by Phyllis Shindler) a short, sad school report: "He does his best, I'm afraid" Playwright Lady Mills tells of the evening when her daughter Hayley aged five appeared in her nightdress at the top of the stairs, as guests were departing and said in the startled silence, "Mummy, my heart has stopped".

Religious humour has to be treated with care unless it is of a general or universal kind. Thus ballerina Beryl Grey, CBE describes the little girl who before the 1939–45 war was running in haste to school and praying every so often 'Please God, don't make me late'. After tripping and falling, she got up again and said, 'Please God, don't push'.

Jews and Catholics are often the butt of jokes, but appear not to be so offended by them as do people of other religions. It helps to have such tales told by people of the same faith. Thus Lady Longford relates the story of a local Italian priest offering to rescue souls from Purgatory at 25 lire a time. "What do you say to that" asked the Anglican Gladstone indignantly of a famous Catholic priest. The priest replied, "Tell me Mr. Gladstone, what other church would do it at the price?"

Tragedy is thought to be a higher art than comedy, perhaps because, unless we are loved by the gods, we all become 'acquainted with grief'.

Socrates regarded life as a preparation for death, but to many people with no belief in an afterlife or other consolation, death is the supreme tragedy. It is the final unavoidable goodbye, *The Big Sleep* as Raymond Chandler called it, into which some unhappy people want to sink, even before their time, to escape the pain of wakefulness.

Humour uplifts the spirit. Write it (and the skill can be learnt largely by trial and error), and fulfil a twofold task. Your comedy and wit adds joy to the lives of your readers, you give comfort to unseen people burdened with sorrow and (a bonus) could even get paid for doing so.

Writing a Novel

The subjects that most concern readers are usually money, royalty, sex or religion. A good opening sentence is therefore 'My God,' said the Duchess to her lover, 'They have stolen my jewels.' But novels need more than a good opening. EM Forster in *Aspects of the Novel*, said they need backbone too. And the backbone of a novel is plot.

The king died and then the queen died is a story: a narrative of events in a time sequence. If that story has causality: the king died and the queen died of grief, we have a plot. A novel needs a mixture of plot, incident, characters and theme, though much published work lacks them.

The best plots are often to be found in novels of a particular genre: romantic, crime, historic, thrillers. Thus we have the aga sagas, crime in the courtroom and sex in the cowshed. Sometimes the agent arranges an auction among publishers for the rights to new novels that fit into the genre slot. Michael Ridpath was a (first) novelist who underwent this happy lottery with his book about the stock exchanges of the USA and the UK. Called *Free to Trade* it became Hard to Read towards the end when the author appeared to be getting enmeshed in his creature's machinations.

30 Ways To Make Money – IN WRITING

'Literary' works that depend for appeal on the excellence of their writing are becoming rarer. This is partly because advertising, say, a romantic novel, is easier and more fruitful than one with a 'general' appeal (unless the latter comes from a well known pen).

If a novel is labelled romantic, readers know the kind of book they are buying or borrowing. They choose Barbara Cartland or Catherine Cookson because they know what they are getting and like it. Similarly with the historical novel, a field in which many writers excel. Indeed, Pat Barker's description in *The Ghost Road* of the 1914–16 battlefields may well have helped her to win the 1995 Booker Prize against stiff competition.

So unless you are convinced of your writing excellence (and why not – most writers have such a conviction without a First in English or a doctorate in 19th century deathbed scenes), the best way to get your novel published is to aim for a specific market, conditioned perhaps by your own kind of reading.

The romantic novel often acts as an outlet for women writers, in the same way as spy, thriller or adventure stories are largely dominated by men. But men or women, young or old, who have the skill to hold readers, can enter any field of literary endeavour that pleases them. In fact the first joint prizewinners of a competition initiated by Romantic novelist Mary Wibberley for either the first 100 words of a romantic novel OR of the first encounter between hero and heroine, turned out to be men writing under women's pseudonyms.

Her own 'Blueprint for Success', as she calls it, lists 10 factors that lead towards a publishable romance. They are motivation without which you cannot begin; enthusiasm which makes you feel for your characters; and organisation. On the latter point, Mary Wibberley suggests you make a list of what you need for a day's writing, and check that you have all those requirements when you begin to write.

She suggests also that you should have a feeling for words; curiosity; enough imagination to weave ideas into stories; able to take criticism while remaining optimistic and sure that you are going to succeed. You need research to ensure that your descriptions of people, places and dates are accurate enough not to annoy the reader. He or she may wish to suspend belief while they are reading your book, but that doesn't mean they welcome gross inaccuracies. However, don't let research become an end in itself.

Some writers go to great lengths to make sure that their description of a town, a mountain or a person is as true to life as they can make it. But the mention of tigers in an early Tarzan book featuring Africa (where they are not native to the land) did not prejudice Edgar Rice Burroughs' success. If your novel has pace and readability you can get away with murder, theoretically speaking, and romance too.

You also need concentration. Mary Wibberley describes how she wrote one of the best scenes in her book *Laird of Gaela* when her two young children were at home, each with two friends. Leaving them with orange juice and biscuits in the kitchen, she told them she was going into her study, and they were only to shout at her, "if it's an emergency".

She wrote steadily for three hours immune to the sound of mini-elephants up the stairs, Red Indian shrieks throughout the house, and the rain swirling outside. Could you write on like that? I certainly couldn't but if you can, there's hope for you as a novelist yet.

Other tips for romantic novelists are to show the antagonism between hero and heroine early, not to have too many characters, and to keep to the book length that seems, judging by other works, most favoured by the publisher.

For crime and detective novels, get the foul deed done as early as possible, dream up a memorable detective, even if he or she isn't Sherlock Holmes, Morse, Detective Inspector Wexford, Miss Silver or Miss Marple, and keep the number of people in the story to a minimum. Inject tension in the first pages and let enlightenment come by degrees. Remembering Barbara Pym's delicious novels and how she languished for 16 years without any of her work being published, it may be wise to keep your rejected manuscripts. You (or yours) may be able to work them over later. Number your pages as you proceed. A wind or child may upset the whole lot. Keep copies of what you send out and get on with the next job.

For the writing of any kind of novel (literary, crime, detective, romance, spy), a useful suggestion comes from Dianne Doubtfire. I first met Dianne many years ago at the only Writers' summer school I ever managed to get to. We both had books published in the following year.

Winston Clewes was lecturing on the novel. Dianne asked him how best she could begin her own. He told her to make a list numbering 1–30. Against number 1 was the opening of the novel. Number 30 was the end. In between, other developments could be planned, or altered, as the story developed. See if this system works for you. Unless you write a best seller your rewards for novel writing are not likely to be high, but working little and often will mean a reasonable income for a long time to come, with the Public Lending Right providing an extra sweetener.

The Short Story

A short story has one obvious advantage for anybody hoping to make money in writing: it is short, not more than 5,000–6,000 words at most. Even if the whole thing has to be rewritten over and over again, that 'wasted' time and effort cannot be compared with the loss involved in discarding a novel. And the 'wasted' time is often a useful learning process.

You can shorten that learning time, and reduce your 'failures' by realising that almost all short stories have a 'linear' plot: that is, a character in conflict and his solution to that problem. A person wants to achieve some aim; there is an obstacle in the way. By solving the problem, the writer holds the reader.

The predicament or obstacle can be quite ordinary: a person goes to a restaurant, wines rather too well, and on leaving puts on the wrong raincoat. Not until he is on his way home, puts his hand into his pocket and finds a letter there, does he realise he is wearing the wrong coat. What does he do with the letter and the coat?

Read some of the 'greats' and see how they deal with characters, problems and their resolution. Does Maupassant's story *The Necklace* fit in with the definition of a linear plot? And what about *The Juggler,* by Anatole France?

For more modern examples, contrast Somerset Maugham's

sophistication and craftsmanship with the equally well crafted stories of Katharine Mansfield, though her backgrounds are so different. Read Saki's dryly malicious stories about aunts, animals and children, or Salinger's about young people in a particular decade *(Franny and Zooey; For Esme with Love* and *Squalor).*

Read Muriel Spark for the delicious zany quality of her writing, her mordant humour; Malamud and Bellow for their portrayal of Jewish characters. Penelope Lively, Booker prizewinner, has also written some penetrating short stories, almost like parables, though the quality is somewhat uneven. If you like detective tales, Ruth Rendell's short stories are for some readers even better than her novels. Francis King, too, is worth studying for the compassion he shows to his characters.

James Joyce's tales of Dublin conjure up such a real picture of the city and its people you can almost see them. And you can hear, too, that wonderful sermon on Hell, which came off even better when adapted for the stage.

Science Fiction has its own masters. Based on the linear plot, the story takes place in a different world. (CS Lewis in *Perelandra, The Silent Planet.*) And if you think science fiction is unintelligible, get hold of a copy of *Flowers for Algernon* by D. Keyes. It was made into the film, *Charlie.*

Written in the first person in the form of a diary, it tells of Charlie, a mentally retarded person who is part of a research project to heighten intelligence. A mouse has the same injection and its progress is reflected in Charlie's own. Charlie falls in love with his teacher and then, horrified, sees the general mental deterioration of the mouse, and knows his turn will come. The author won the Hugo Prize for science fiction, and when asked how he had managed to produce such a gem, said that if he knew how, he'd do it again.

The Short Story

Beginners sometimes find it hard to differentiate between an incident and a plot. A plot shows cause and conflict: a lead character wants to do or get something which he cannot because of psychological or physical obstacles in the way. He resolves the problem by some logical but unexpected solution. An incident merely describes an event or happening without moving to any conclusion.

If you find it hard to start, don't resort to time wasting pursuits like tidying up the desk, playing about with the computer graphics, fiddling with the biro or phoning up colleagues for a chat. Think of short cuts to putting words on paper. Ask yourself the question 'What if. . . ?' L. A. G. Strong had another plan. He took three objects, chosen at random, and tried to put them into a sequence to make a plot. It didn't always work, but it was a start. Overheard snatches of conversation on bus or train can often be the beginning of a character, the start of a plot.

Places, too, may have a 'feel' about them: haunting, romantic or menacing, which can start you off. Or take a background of movement: a caving expedition, a ride on the Underground, people trapped in a boat, a lift, put in your lead (or even minor) character, and see what happens to them. You can take this from the front end, with your readers not knowing how the story will finish, or you can take some well known ending to a disaster, and tell it from the beginning. Most unusual incidents can be turned into stories.

Hook the reader on the first line. Suggest something is happening or about to happen, or that you are going to unfold a different world. Another way to hook readers is by the title, contrasting it with the opening lines (but publishers may alter your title). You can give your characters unusual names, dream up witticisms, or add something that can only be called style. When you have rounded off your characters, developed and resolved their problem, quickly end the story.

With detective or adventure short stories, everything, including characterisation, must take second place to action. The emphasis is on structure, the way the plot unfolds, the building up of tension. This means that if you can devise plots and puzzles you may be able to write very acceptable stories of this kind. You do not have to be particularly gifted with words, as long as the reader appreciates that what you are saying is, in effect, 'Hold me tight, baby. I'm your link with the action'.

Your stories can be short or long. As an example of a very, very short detective story, read Henry VI, Part II Act 2 Scene 1, lines 59–160 beginning with "Enter Townsman of St. Alban's crying 'A Miracle'" and ending with a speech by Gloucester "from whence they came." Who plays the detective? What are the clues?

Finally, where are the best markets for the sale of your efforts? The answer is in the women's magazines. Competition is tough, and the standard often surprisingly high. More of the Sunday magazines are now publishing short stories too, and literary journals provide opportunities for the experimentalist. The *Raconteur* magazine, a collection of short stories published quarterly at £16, is a newcomer on the scene with some excellent prizewinning short stories (44 Gray's Inn Road, London WC1X 8LR).

Other outlets (short stories and poetry) are *Ambit* 17 Priory Gardens London N6 5QY; *Sunk Island Review* PO Box 74, Lincoln LN1 1QG; and *Iron Magazine* 3 Marden Terrace, North Shields, Northumberland NE30 4PD (poetry, fiction and graphics).

Chance your arm. Every brilliant author was once a beginner.

Radio Scripts

It is usually harder for a part time writer to achieve success in the world of radio than in magazine journalism. There are fewer outlets. If your script fails to find favour with the broadcasting companies, where else can you place it? By contrast, if two publishers don't like your novel, you have the choice of at least another hundred, and there are thousands of magazine and newspaper outlets for articles.

But money can be made in broadcasting, even by a beginner. So many writers have been lured by the charismatic attraction of TV that radio producers go all out to encourage writers who show even a glimmer of talent. And unless you make the effort, how will you ever know whether you have a flair for this kind of work?

Established writers often have no desire to try a new medium. Why should they give up certain earnings for uncertain ones? They generally enter the radio world to adapt works they have already produced in another form. The beginner with no published work to his credit has nothing to lose and much to gain by attempting a piece for radio.

And though there are still only comparatively few broadcasting channels, those channels must have new voices, new writers. Every day and all day the waves are working. The demand is immense. Quizzes, panel games, documentaries, memoirs, talks, how to cook, fish, sew, knit, furnish a home – all is grist to the radio mill. But a word of caution. If you think you have a good idea write it down in some formalised way. THERE IS NO COPYRIGHT IN IDEAS.

Study radio programmes to see what is currently being produced. All the newspapers now produce weekly radio supplements in addition to their daily programmes with their pick of the night, day or week. See what attracts listeners (and viewers). Single out a slot which attracts you, whether it be talks, short stories or plays. See whether they are targeted for a special audience such as people at home, car drivers, the retired or disabled. Listen critically. Can you do as well or better?

For talks, dictating rather than writing is speedier and gives a better idea of the sound effect. Send in a cassette if you prefer, particularly if you have a good voice, but the contract you get, if any, will be based on a written script approved by the producer.

For sketches and sitcom pieces you need, as with straight plays, a beginning or premise, then the complications and the resolution. Send your manuscript to the appropriate department of the radio station you are trying to besiege. To write for an invisible audience, imagine you have a listener sitting before you, and are chatting to him or her about your ideas or experiences. Don't be formal. If your script proves acceptable, not an unknown event, you will be asked along to the studio. Practise on a tape recorder first to get an idea of how the talk will sound, and how long it will last.

You will be able to hear, and remedy, any trace of nervousness in your voice. Practice makes perfect in this case, and familiarity with the content will give you confidence when you have to speak. Don't worry too much about the sound. Engineers can do all manner of things to your voice without losing the essential timbre which makes it uniquely yours.

The most important question when talking (not for plays because actors will take over your script) is will your audience be able to understand what you say? Accents are attractive, but not if they are so 'thick' as to be unintelligible. If such is your own case, you may have to let some other reader give your talk. Pitch and resonance do not matter. Rely on the sound engineers and the producer. They will give you lots of tips to make your voice come over well and tell you, for example, how far to keep away from the microphone, not to make unnecessary movements when you are speaking, to avoid if you can the sibilant hiss of 's' and the pop of 'p'.

This was not the situation when I wrote my first talk. In it I had mimicked some Cockney dialogue. The producer liked the dialogue very much indeed, unfortunately better than the talk. He said he would like me to write some Cockney scripts. Could I do them? Now, more experienced, I would reply 'Of course' (presuming I wanted to write them anyway). Then, naïve, and almost overcome at being asked to the portals of Broadcasting House at all, I said modestly I didn't think so. End of chance to become a big noise perhaps, and almost end of chapter except that I was sufficient of a Cockney to write later to the BBC for expenses.

They replied that it was not their policy to reimburse unsuccessful writers for their attendance, but they paid up just the same. So there were two lessons to be gained from this experience. The first is that anybody who wants to make money in writing for radio must be prepared (if not actually able or willing) to write about anything. That is why, at a later date, when my accent proved unacceptable for the German radio, and I was asked to write scripts for youngsters learning English, I volunteered with alacrity, though I had never attempted such a thing before. Produced with little handbooks for schools, the broadcasts were a great success, and went on the air weekly for more than two years.

The second lesson has all the backing of St. Luke behind it, namely that the labourer is worthy of his hire. You will discover that radio, however stimulating, is not the highest paid medium for which to write. In TV you may be plied with drinks before a programme begins, to help you 'relax'. In radio, it is said, doubtless with little truth, that you have practically to faint to get a glass of water.

As a beginner to broadcasting, you're not likely to be able to command much in the way of a fee but don't forget St. Luke entirely. Writers, in common with other earners, have to distinguish between what is due in justice and what in charity, even if they are working part time or from their own home. In the beginning, you have to prove your worth to learn your trade.

Take the rate that is offered and be glad of acceptance and getting broadcast. At least, it is very good publicity. Later on, as in all spheres, when you have achieved some success, you may be able to negotiate better terms. They may not greatly improve your own lot, but will help those who come after you and have not so much clout as you.

In spite of its comparatively poor monetary reward compared with more glamorous TV, radio with its sense of immediacy is, for many writers, the most exciting of all media in which to express their ideas.

Radio Plays

Good at dialogue? Poor at description? Do you more easily hear rather than see a scene in your mind? Then have a shot at radio plays. Your chances as an untried practitioner are far better in this market than live theatre: 400 hours of new plays and adaptations are broadcast every year in addition to readings. New talent is encouraged by regional, national and local radio stations and a free leaflet *Writing Plays for Radio* can be obtained from the Chief Producer, Plays (Radio Drama), BBC, Broadcasting House, Portland Place, London W1A 1AA.

Good ideas are also welcome, whether for a serial or for single plays. Put your idea into a written format, for example the list of characters and a brief description, with sample script. If it is liked, you will be asked to complete the script, though not with any assurance of final acceptance. If the idea is still liked, experienced writers may take over, especially with a serial production. You will get paid for your idea, and given credit for it, alongside that of the person who actually writes the script.

One big advantage for the beginner in writing radio plays is that settings may be anywhere, events happen in any world, past, present or future, with no need for descriptions. Everything is told through sound. Expense therefore is not the prime consideration as it often has to be with plays for television or live theatre. That gives you, the beginner, a better chance to break into this market.

Do not have a large cast of 'voices'. Your audience must be able to distinguish easily between them from the speech and characteristics of the actors alone. Crowd scenes with their own hum of sounds can add to the play's realism at minimal production cost.

Read (or see) the plays of the 'greats'. Note how they stick to a theme. For example in *Macbeth* it is "ambition that o'er leaps itself". Ibsen's *The Doll's House* is almost equally powerful, with compelling characters, and concise dialogue held together by a story that never wanders from its theme.

The main principles to remember in writing radio plays are similar to those of the live theatre or television. They are the three Cs of CHARACTER, CONFLICT and CRISIS. Action, which is an important part of television drama, comes across in radio by different sounds (crowds cheering, waves breaking, cars starting, doors shutting, etc.).

On the other hand, radio does not give the same opportunity for actors as the live theatre does. There are no close-ups, no chance of meaningful eye glances; no view of anybody's tears – the breaking heart must sob, not cry silently; fighters must come to blows that can be heard, moving vehicles never move silently. This does not mean your characters cannot come alive. Your listener should identify with and be moved by them; feel the crisis, big or small, they have to resolve.

The length of a radio play, at 30, 60 or more rarely 90 minutes, is much shorter than one for a live theatre audience, so get your listeners quickly 'hooked'. That is not always easy for they are made up of very different people: they may be driving a car on a long boring journey; invalids in a hospital bed; disabled people in wheelchairs; mothers (or even fathers nowadays) at home with small children.

There is also a very large and important audience: blind people, who depend upon you and other writers like you for entertainment, amusement and information. Entertain them, mystify them, but above all, hold them in the first few seconds.

To get the attention of the audience it sometimes pays to introduce the end of a radio play first. One of the characters can begin with a couple of lines like 'That day we went for our picnic, I had no idea my husband meant to murder me...' You then introduce sounds such as gulls wheeling, which describe the picnic place and fade out to the real opening of the play. The ingenious writer can think of many such openings. The main point to remember is that their object is to grab the listener, and hold him by the throat until he is hooked.

You are not meant to give the entire game away in the first few lines, so that there is no incentive to hear more. Hold your listener with only infrequent lessenings of your grip until the final fade out. There is no time to allow, as in live theatre, for the audience to settle themselves while the curtains are drawn, the butler brings in the breakfast and remarks that it is a pleasant morning, sir.

Get into the action straightaway. Give explanations later. Your actors won't be able to 'feel' any audience response and adapt their lines accordingly. Words and action must rivet, or promise to rivet, your audience in the opening seconds. Do not as a beginner be too concerned with 'stage' directions. Provided a radio play is legibly typed, the layout is not vitally important. Producers are more interested in a script's contents than its looks. You can type the names of the characters in red if you prefer, set them either at the left or, as is the American way, in the centre of the page.

But there are some general rules worth knowing. They have proved satisfactory because they help directors to calculate quickly the playing time of a script. Action, dialogue and direction are kept to a single $3^1/2$ inch column on the right half of the page. Directions, if any to the left. Names of CHARACTERS are written in capitals and underlined.

Anything the writer wishes to include by way of notes is in CAPITALS. Dialogue is in lower case type, single spaced with double spacing between speeches and treble spacing between dialogue and directions.

Each page is numbered twice. At the top is the page number of the appropriate part (for example, II – 4 indicates the fourth page of the second part). At the foot is the total page number of the script starting from the first page of the first part. The scene, set and time should be clearly indicated but there is no need to give specific details like the kind of furniture in the sitting room, unless it is vital to the plot.

In front of the script, give a list of the characters with a brief line about them. If you wish you can outline the theme of your play in not more than thirty words.

Now forget the mechanics. And get on with the action.

Live Theatre

If you think you can make money by writing a play for live theatre, think again. Remember Noel Coward's lyric with its advice to Mrs. Worthington about putting her daughter on the stage: don't. Such negative advice prefaces this chapter because (i) it will not stop anybody with the desire and ambition to write a stage play and (ii) it is sometimes good to be aware of the odds stacked against you.

It is not easy for an unknown or comparatively unknown writer to find a management willing to look favourably on his play. Perhaps the best way to get into the market, therefore, is to try to persuade one of the many amateur drama groups, fringe or repertory theatres to present it. Most important in the group of UK theatres who still actively seek plays from new writers are the English Stage Company, the Royal Court Theatre, London SW1 8AS.

The Soho Theatre Company (0171 262 7907) also gives an ear to new plays and playwrights and welcomes unsolicited scripts. These are read by a professional panel who write a detailed critical report. The company offers workshop facilities, including rehearsed reading and platform performances for promising playwrights and sometimes the opportunity to discuss with actors and directors ways to develop their work.

If a play is liked, a director or other influential person will try to use his powers of persuasion to get it produced, or maybe ask the author to make necessary changes in the script. Cockpit Theatre, Gateforth Street NW8 8EH, Hammersmith's Lyric Theatre (0181 741 0824) and the Bush Theatre at Shepherds Bush (0171 602 3708) are also happy to look at unsolicited scripts; the latter produces six premières a year. Writers who are being commissioned or encouraged by a theatre company may be eligible for financial assistance. Get a copy of the brochure *Schemes for Writers and Theatre Companies* from the Arts Council of England, 14 Great Peter Street, London SW1P 3NQ.

Reports of recent productions in local and national newspapers and *The Stage* also indicate possible markets for the wonderful drama that you have just completed. Alternatively you can try a literary agent, though not everyone will want to take you on. Show that you are an active worker in some dramatic society – scene shifting, directing, acting – all help to display your knowledge of live theatre and therefore to give some credibility to your own play.

If you can make it with a 'live' script, what are the rewards? Rates for top writers are negotiable. Agreements for theatre writers have been negotiated by the Writers' Guild of Great Britain. These agreements cover some 200 theatres. Copies of those for theatre writers can be obtained from the Guild at 430 Edgware Road, London W2 1EH. The Guild negotiates minimum terms for writers in all media, updated from time to time, and those agreements form the basis of individual contracts signed by members.

Sometimes grants and bursaries are available to encourage

young playwrights in their writing development. If a play does take off in a West End Theatre, the sky is the limit with 4%–10% of box office receipts accruing to the author, depending on the contract.

Additionally you may get repeat rights as small regional theatres put on your work. A new market is developing in published texts. These are often on sale in the foyer of a theatre where the play is being shown. John Osborne's *Look Back in Anger*, produced as a stage play in 1956, published as a text in 1957, was 30 years later still selling more than 20,000 copies. Harold Pinter's *Caretaker* (1960) did nearly as well.

So how does one begin in this market of rich rewards and dismal disappointments? Are there any lessons to be learned in how to write a play and make an income from such work? Playwright Edward Albee starts by putting his characters in a situation different from the one he is thinking about. If they behave normally in that altered situation, he knows he is on to a winner and starts to write.

Some critics believe that a play, like a story, should have a beginning, a middle and an end, and suggest that it should start as near the end as possible. The main ingredient of a successful play is that the writer must know what it is about. This is not how his audience sees it. They think of bits of dialogue, the scenes, costume, style.

Recall the work of some 20th century playwrights and you will see that this is true: the lighthearted romances of Noel Coward *(French Without Tears)* , and their equally lighthearted, often brittle but sometimes memorable dialogue ('Anyone for Tennis?'). Think of Pinter's plays and their quirky dissolute characters bantering repartee with a dark hint of menace. Many of the lines, with their so pregnant pauses, owed much to the marvellous delivery by Pinter's first wife, Vivien Merchant.

And yet a playwright does not sit down to write marvellous lines; they come from the reaction of characters to one another and the situations in which the playwright puts them. The writer may use similar scenes each time but every play has to have its own structure or backbone. Thus nearly all of Alan Ayckbourn's plays have a domestic setting. Humour is injected throughout, with often a faint air of sadness, a whiff of tragedy at the end. This is not the same as a theme, more in the nature of an idea.

Arthur Miller says that each 'idea' implies a structure peculiar to itself. And for that, as he put it in conversation with Otis Guernsey, of the US Dramatists' Guild Quarterly, " It's essential to be able to identify the main thrust of the work".

Though a playwright begins writing on the page, the work will go on stage. It is not one-to-one communication, but played through a group on stage to a group listening 'out there'. Other forms of communication such as a novel or a book, even a TV play, can be enjoyed by one person. But a play on stage must come alive when performed. If it doesn't, however marvellous the dialogue and scenery, it remains wooden. Audiences pay their money and hope to get some stimulus, some excitement, something worthwhile to think about when they leave the bright lights. Give it to them, with all that you've got.

Song Writing

Writing songs can be a way of earning a living or possibly of making a fortune. Musicals like *Phantom of the Opera, Les Miserables, Starlight Express* and *Cats* have all broken box office records. Yet successes like these begin simply with words and music. So too do the European song contests and records sung by the stars.

You may not possess Richard Stilgoe's unique gift for so aptly setting words to music, but have a musical ear and a flair for 'catchy' phrases. So why not try your hand at writing songs? It may be all hard work, little fun and no 'mon', my son. But how will you know how good (or bad) you are unless you try? The marathon runner who comes last in a race does better than the one who is listed DNF (did not finish), and both have beaten the unlisted one who DNS (did not start). Go in for the ride. Even if your song writing efforts don't hit the jackpot you could become so expert in the field that your work will be sought after and commissioned.

Begin by reading one or two biographies of modern song writers. Look at their methods, then at others, to see how they began. Some start with a title, others with the words. What do you want for your beginning point: a melody or the line? Either way, the type of song (that is its style) and the form for composing it are essential ingredients when you begin.

If you are writing to order, and this can happen quite early in a lyrical career, you must keep carefully to the project specifications for the overall piece. You should also be acutely aware of your target audience.

When you are not working on a commissioned piece, find out how to promote your work, Develop a knowledge of the industry's commercial market place so that you make an income in this chosen field. Outlets for the song writer can include several of the following: lyrics for composers; song writing for performers; film scores; library music; documentaries; carols; TV themes; operas; pop records and arrangements; musicals and theatrical productions.

It is not easy for beginners to market song lyrics on their own. Music publishers like to hear complete works. If you cannot compose the music to go with your words, team up with someone who can. If you have no friends or contacts, advertise in the local or music press or join a society like the British Academy of Songwriters, Composers and Authors (BASCA, 34 Hanway Street, London W1P 9DE).

Draw up a marketing plan. Call or write to the most appropriate people. They will include library music houses who should be asked in what areas they need more material. Create some demos for them. A demo is a demonstration track of words and music, for example, piano and voice.

The A & R (Artist and Repertoire) Department of record companies is in charge of hearing new talent. They may be busy, or have other reasons for not seeing you. In this case, send a package with a tape containing two or three titles, a letter, CV and a stamped addressed envelope for their return.

Follow this through with phone calls until you have a response. The Music Publishers' Association (MPA), 3rd floor, Strandgate, 18–20 York Buildings, London WC2N 6JU) has a regularly updated members' list.

Try the performing venues. These vary enormously from pubs to concert halls. They have their own promoters and if you call them at the venue and inform them of your project, the usually very helpful promoters will give you the most suitable contact for your package. Alternatively, perform yourself. Talent scouts go round looking for new singers and composers and it may be your lucky night. You can try also the Songwriter Showcases and similar events held in the London area. Get details from the MPA.

Trying to interest orchestras, theatrical or operatic producers is usually attempted only by students of music. Study the type of works that find most favour. Look up the venue, find out the resident producer/director and briefly describe your work to them. If they are not interested, or there are no suitable projects for you, they may be able to recommend your work to others, or give you contacts that may help you. Contact the Society for the Promotion of New Music, West Heath Studios, 174 Mill Lane, London NW6 1TB.

The publishing, theatrical and film industries produce booklets and monthly leaflets with information on future events, the artists and projects that want new material, as well as film and theatrical producers and directors looking for participants to work on current or forthcoming productions.

Some publishers are extremely helpful. They know which particular artists, companies, film and TV houses are looking for material and may even give you initial financial support for your songs, register your works, and later collect your royalties.

Record companies and potential clients tend to take more notice of publishing houses than individuals, rather as a book recommended by a literary agent is usually more acceptable to a publisher than one from an unknown name.

For TV themes, write and send packages to the major TV houses. Look out also for the names of individual film makers. Forward details and packages to their directors, but find out first the name of the appropriate addressee. If your work is not returned in spite of enclosing a stamped envelope, knowing to whom it was sent may help you recover it, though recorded delivery is better (but dearer).

The payment for commercial sound recording is usually 8.5% of the dealer price of each sound carrier, shared between publisher and authors of the work. Percentages for public performances and broadcasts are detailed in any agreement. These rights are traditionally assigned to the Performing Rights Society and the royalties from them paid direct to composer/author/publisher. The royalty on printed music is normally 10% of the retail selling price. Different works such as featured or non-featured music, TV and radio music, the a and b sides of records, jingles, signature tunes, theatrical works, may earn different rates. The PRS also has different rates and fees depending on where works are performed, for example in a place of public performance, auditorium, TV or radio station.

Copyright in musical compositions comprises the right of publication in print and sale of printed copies; the right of public performance and the right to use the work to make records, sound films or other similar contrivances. It is therefore very far reaching. If you are not eligible to join the Performing Rights Society – which is the situation when you have not yet had anything accepted, commercially published and recorded, on TV, radio, or film – take steps to protect the copyright of your work.

Get a form from Stationers Hall in Ave Maria Lane, London EC4M 7DD, fill it in and have your work/manuscript witnessed by a responsible person such as a lawyer or bank manager before sending it off. The cost for registering is £30 + VAT for an individual, £50 + VAT for a company.

If your work is likely to be or has been broadcast, recorded or played publicly, the Performing Rights Society are the people to approach. They will collect the fees due to you each time your work is played, and forward the royalties to you. Address: 29–33 Berners Street, London W1P 4AA.

Jingles

A jingle is a piece of music that accompanies an advertisement or commercial on the radio or television. It is also the name for a musical ident, that is a piece of music/lyric which announces a station, programme, event or person.

Jingles are most commonly used on the TV screen to support a short film commercial promoting a product or service. The amount of work taken to produce this end product is considerable, though it might last a mere 30 seconds on screen. Hours of labour and many people are involved in its making from the initial idea to completion. Substantial sums too, not least of which is the cost of air time, go towards its production.

But the great joy of writing for this big but specialised market is the pressure to produce such a variety of 'shapes'. Every company or client to whom you can sell your ideas and your words has specific needs which will be spelt out when you get a 'brief'. These different needs are very challenging, and mean that your work must be constantly changing and adapting. If you are going to make money by writing jingles, you must constantly be able to create 'fresh pieces' which will stand out above others, year after year. When you have established yourself with one or two successful pieces, projects and ideas may come from clients. You will then have to discipline yourself to compress lyrical and musical thoughts into a very tiny slot, and do it with style.

The skill in writing jingles is to highlight the advertisement with exactly the right word or sound that makes your product more successful than a competitor's. Your jingle has to get the viewer's attention, appeal to his/her emotions, entertain him/her and make him/her more receptive to a repetitive message. The jingle has to avoid 'overkill', for if viewers get tired of hearing it and switch to another channel, the message is lost.

How do you start in this musical jungle of jingles? Look for music publishers who welcome disks and tapes. Most will only accept lyrics with music, so if you cannot compose the music you will have to find a partner who can.

Names and addresses of music production houses that might represent you can be found in the *Creative Handbook*, published at £115 annually by Reed Information Services, Windsor Court, East Grinstead House, West Sussex RH19 1XA (01342 326972). Also listed in its pages are advertising agencies and TV producers. Or start with any of the agency names in *Campaign*. This magazine covers the whole of the mass communications field particularly advertising, marketing and the media. Radio stations producing their own idents and commercials are another outlet. So too are public relations and marketing companies. Many of them advertise in *Marketing Week*.

Contact your chosen market with a showreel containing as much variety and material as possible. Give them demos, masters, songs etc. Get hold of some advertising agency scripts. Old ones will do. Practise with these scripts to write your own

Jingles

commercials. Send them in with a stamped addressed envelope. Or as a way of testing your own ability, video commercial tracks without their sound, and put your own composition on to them.

This effort should also impress the agency (or other client) to whom you are hoping to sell your work. That work has to interpret the mood, market and feel of the audience to whom it is directed. Try composing three different pieces of music to the same film. This will show how responsive the music and lyrics are to the mood and events that take place in the campaign.

Create a CV to accompany any of these efforts, even if you have not previously done much, or any, professional work before. The CV can at least reveal your versatility, by presenting the kind of work you have previously done, and the names of previous employers or clients. The closer the latter are to the song writing or entertainment industry, the better.

Send off the CV with your cassette or disk to the people from whom you hope to get a commission, wait 10 days, and then ring them up until they agree to give you an appointment, a guideline as to whom you should be talking, or return your work. Ask them if they are, or ever will be, interested in your work. Your approach is very important. Shrinking violets do not survive in this field.

Your potential clients are receiving hundreds of calls like yours all the time. Yours must be the one they remember. If you are successful, you will get a brief. This gives the guidelines within which the jingle must be written. A meeting is held with the advertising agency, production company, sometimes the client proper. The TV producer and copywriter from the agency are usually also present.

A story board explains the brief. It shows the outline of the film content on one side and the dialogue and music on the other. The length of the commercial is agreed. Age groups and target audience are discussed in great detail from research already undertaken. So is the mood of the campaign. The words and lyrics are looked over and checked to make sure they scan with the music. Various styles of music are discussed to verify the client's viewpoint (for example, do they prefer male or female voices for the lyrics?). Sometimes the brief is 'open'. This gives you more flexibility.

Finally, fees are discussed. Do the clients want the cheaper 'demo' or will they buy a dearer 'pilot' track? A 'demo' is a rough basic music/words track with, say, voice and piano. A 'pilot' track is a more sophisticated upmarket demo carrying more instrumentation, but still not the fully fledged, composed, finished work. This is the point when you will have to consider how much your work is worth. If you are a poor judge of your own ability, or a poor negotiator, get an agent, or advice on the going rate from the Musicians' Union (MU), 60/62 Clapham Road, London SW9 0JJ.

Films

Other than possessing a modicum of good looks or a striking image, making money by writing for films is just like becoming a film star. Both depend on luck, ambition, contacts and talents, unfortunately in that order. As such a few films are produced in the UK each year, put yourself in a position from which luck can operate. Start by joining the British Film Institute, 21 Stephen Street W1P 2LN. Its library and information service contains the world's largest collection of material relating to film and TV. Membership including a monthly newsletter costs £11.95 and for a library pass £15. Technology now makes film writing and editing a much easier task; you can direct your family and see the result of your camera work with all its imperfections on the television screen.

Courses in cultural or film studies are sometimes available as part of an English degree. Bournemouth University offers a full programme in Script Writing for Film and TV; the University of Leeds has a one year MA course in Film and TV Scriptwriting (fiction); the courses at the University of East Anglia for Creative Writing (founded by Malcolm Bradbury) offer tuition in script and screen writing. Thames University has a one year course 'aimed at those wanting to explore creative script writing in a small group with personal supervision' (Thames University) St. Mary's Road London W5 5RF.

If you are too hard up for courses, an income through involvement in film could come from community projects. They describe their activities on TV or in newspapers, and seek applicants to join them as researchers, actors, directors and script writers. Some jobs overlap, as budgets tend to be of the shoestring variety.

Regional Arts Councils and local authorities fund some schemes for the amateur film maker and script writer. Check with your local authority, or write to the Arts Council in your area. For other grants and subsidies to potential film makers, consult also the Directory of Grant Making Trusts published by the Charities Aid Foundation, or the Department of Trade and Industry. If you set up your own group, you might be able to get some assistance from the National Lottery Fund. You will have to make out a good case.

Another way to get help in film making, script writing and ancillary work, is to find 10 like-minded citizens. If half of them are of pensionable age, and their project helps the community, the group may be eligible for a fairly large grant from the New Horizons Trust, a charitable trust run by city stockbrokers.

So much for courses and grants. Now to the practice. When submitting film scripts, put title, page number, exterior (EXT) or interior (INT) and set (LIVING ROOM) in capitals on each page. Characters are always in capitals, with actions, dialogue, description, instructions (cut/close up) in lower case. Estimate one page of A4 script to one minute of time, put your name and address on front and end pages, and unlike any other form of manuscript, bind the copy. Kemp's *Film and Year Book* and *The Writer and The Screen* (Wolf Rilla) give fuller details on film writing including how to lay on scripts, the meanings of different types of instruction, and the processes of shooting and editing.

More important than the mechanics of script writing are motivation, a thick skin and an understanding of the economy of film. Think of that scene in *The African Queen* showing Bogart and Hepburn, desperate and despondent, immured hopelessly in the reeds, completely unaware how near they are to open water. Then comes the brilliant following shot: an aerial view of the downpour that fills the rivers; and of their boat floating out to the open sea within sight of their target. Wonderful stuff!

Or there is Polanski's *Compulsion:* the camera pans round the landing, the people, the flat with its debris, and ticking clock, to focus on a photo of the murderer as a schoolgirl. The magnification increases until all we see is her eye looking askance at her father. The eye grows to a terrifying blur, and the film ends. And what about that moving shot in *All Quiet On The Western Front,* where the soldier is killed as he reaches out to touch a butterfly?

As for motivation, here are two examples. A neighbour's son was madly keen to become part of a film making group. He got a tiny job at even tinier pay when Steven Spielberg was in England. He learnt that a film was to be shot in India, saved up everything he had, and flew out to the set.

Experienced and willing to do almost anything, he was allowed around the set. Though a ratio of Indian to foreign actors had to be maintained he proved so useful and reliable he earned his passage, became the lowest of the 'gaffers', and climbed gradually upwards. When I attended a movie première in a Leicester Square theatre, his name was in the list of credits.

The second story concerns the Hong Kong film *Father & Son* with stars Shek Lui and Cheng Yu-or. Based in China but with the universal theme of family ties, it shows director Allen Fong growing up in the sixties. As a boy he defies parental disapproval of his film ambitions. The poorly paid father wants more for his son. But only the daughter works hard and gets good academic results.

The boy, expelled from several schools, sells his books to buy film, and his father who, in his own way, dearly loves the son, destroys the camera in a quarrel. The hardworking sister cannot go to university but has to find a husband to pay for her brother's entry to a US college.

You are a pretty girl, the father says. You can surely find a nice boy friend. Not too rich, he urges her, because rich young men are unreliable. The girl does as she is bid. We see a set in which the prospective suitor is accepted by the father. They discuss realistically the cost of the boy's college fees at $10,000 a year. 'For how long?' sensibly asks the young man. And then the son gets up from the table, quarrelling with his father.

The film ends with the family at the airport seeing the boy off to the US. For young men, the film shows that you get what you want if you want it hard enough. Older men will see it as showing that the son has no appreciation of the sacrifices made by his parents. How women, young or old, will react. . . do I need to say?

If you want something badly enough, you usually manage to achieve that aim. What you have to ask yourself is whether the end result is worth the price, or can you achieve the same result in perhaps a cheaper or less damaging way?

Teaching

When you have made some money in writing, you can boost your income by teaching others. Local authority and private organisations run regular courses throughout the year. They also put on weekend and summer schools where beginners learn basic writing skills, and through lectures, seminars and workshops, more advanced students produce work that sells.

If you have any published work to your name, or qualifications in English Literature/Language, apply to the local authority in your area, saying you wish to set up a Creative Writing course. Give it another name, if you prefer, like Writing for Fun and Profit, or Successful Writing for Beginners.

Enclose with your application the best of your publications, and any relevant details of past experience. You will probably be asked to fill in a standard form. On this, allow your imaginative talents full play. If you are appointed by the local authority, the pay will depend on the grading of your subject. It is made on an hourly rate and comes at the end of the month.

The teaching sessions are usually three hours per evening with a 10 minute break, and one evening a term for about 10–12 weeks. Pay even at the lower end of the scale is good enough to make you turn out in the snowy depths of winter, but if insufficient numbers enrol, the class will not start.

It could end, too, if you don't keep students interested enough or they go down with flu, so that numbers drop below the point of no return. To avoid this disaster, end each session on such an upbeat that they all rush to turn out again next week, come hell or high water.

Whether you are taking over an existing course, or setting up your own, find out what your students want. What is their aim in coming on this course? Put such questions down on paper, and ask the students to write down their answers in class. Ask them what newspapers or magazines they regularly read. They come from varied backgrounds, and knowing their favourite reading, books, films, etc. is helpful in adapting the course to their needs.

Stress the voluntary nature of these questions. Whatever the answers, an introduction to basic English skills, and exercises to extend vocabulary never come amiss. Make this the first 'lecture' topic. Give and ask for examples of style: 'writing of such quality that it invites and rewards repeated careful readings' as a report once defined literature.

Thereafter, have a written plan for each period of the remaining weekly sessions so that you cover various aspects of the writer's craft. Hand out a list to your students of books available in the local library. Librarians (helpful clan) will often draw up a book list for you. Give them an idea of your readers' requirements. Ask students, too, for suggestions.

I used to have two postcards with authors in alphabetical order from Stacy Aumonier (excellent plots; craftsmanship) and Arnold Bennett (*The Writer's Craft*. . . practical instruction) to E. H. Young (ability to create a memorable character out of

Teaching

an insignificant woman) and Mary Webb's *Precious Bane* which I noted for 'outstanding descriptive work'. The 42 authors and books on my cards had such comments to encourage their reading by members of the class.

Give self testing questions at the end of each lecture topic. Thus one lecture might be 'ideas and where to find them', or 'ideas: what makes them sell?'. The self testing questions might then be: has your article a market, or is it just a piece of self expression? Is it a collection of random ideas and facts, or has it got an angle? Have you enough background material, or are you researching so much that you will miss your deadline? Is the piece topical? Is it new? Are you aiming for too high a market? It is better to have a small sale from The Rabbit Lover's Newsletter than a rejection from the most prestigious of magazines.

Other lecture topics can be 'Beginnings and Endings', 'Titles', 'Style', 'Markets', and 'Tools of The Trade'. The latter would give an overview of the various technical helps available including the word processor, fax machine, modem, Internet and so on. Producers or retailers of such equipment are often pleased to arrange a demonstration, in the hope of getting a sale or two. Have a word with the principal of the college first.

Get students to write a maximum 1,000 words, and tell them to suggest three markets for their work. They are not in the class, you presume (but you could be wrong), to learn to earn money by writing. Motivate them to do so. One of the most successful of these exercises in a class of my own was on travel.

The headmaster in the class got a piece in *The Times Educational Supplement* on 'What the Travel Brochures Never Reveal', the caretaker's wife, a piece in *The Lady* on The Islands

30 Ways To Make Money – IN WRITING

of Scotland, a pensioner wrote in The *Daily Telegraph* on The Joy of Holidays at Home and an 18 year old a poem in the local newspaper on Journeys of The Mind.

When students get rejections, ask them the following questions:

1. Was your lead interesting? Will the reader want to read on?

2. Can the theme be summarised in a sentence?

3. Are your sentences relevant to that theme, or do they wander, never to return?

4. Does your piece inform, inspire or entertain the reader?

5. Is it an obvious rehash of old material?

6. Check your style. Can it be improved?

7. Have you given figures or facts to prove your points in a form that the reader can understand?

8. Do you end on an upbeat, encapsulate the theme, and leave the reader with a glow of satisfaction, or does the article fizzle out like a damp rocket?

9. Is the manuscript well presented with accurate spelling and clear typing? Does it look attractive?

10. Was it sent out in time?

If you and they can answer 'Yes' to all those questions, it's the editor at fault. Send the piece to somebody more perspicacious.

TV
(With Specimen Script)

Cable and satellite have enormously increased the opportunities for TV writing of all kinds: book adaptations, plays, documentaries, travel, talks, news. Are you bursting with ideas? Have you a good a good ear for dialogue including regional accents, a sense of drama and the ability to visualise a scene? If so, you might well be successful working for the exciting medium of the small screen.

In the past, one of the obstacles to getting work accepted for TV was that if one company did not take your script, there were few other channels you could try. By contrast to these restricted opportunities there were literally hundreds for writers in magazines, newspapers and books.

The huge advance of technology means that many more channels are being added to the air waves. Those channels daily need acceptable material for a particular and preferably mass audience.

So what kind of scripts find favour? The negative advice is that series are usually preferred to single programmes and established characters and settings to new faces. Producers appear also not to view too kindly those scripts that mean sending cameramen and actors on a global tour.

What about panel games? Unfortunately for new writers, ideas for these come in hundreds to the television companies; added to which presenters usually have their own projects for future programmes. Perhaps only five outside submissions a week can be filed away for use.

You might think that with your dynamic personality and catering or horticultural skills, you could devise a programme to show off your talents as cook or gardener, etc. Alas! even a casual survey of the TV screen will show you that there are plenty of such experts around already, and freelance opportunities for competing with them is severely limited.

You could have much better luck with documentaries. These are usually of two kinds: (a) real life stories presented in dramatic form with actors playing the parts of existing people. An example is the 999 series. This format shows the various emergency services or individuals saving the lives of people in dire emergencies who, for example, have fallen over a cliff face, with the tide mounting inexorably near their injured bodies; the fire and ambulance services rescuing somebody trapped under a lorry, in a swamp, or in an air pocket under water; who has fallen down a well or a mountain crevasse and is unable to move.

Good writing in a literary sense is not necessary for these stories: the drama is in the happening itself, the predicament of the person involved before and after their saviours' arrival; the rescuers' thoughts as they work out the best way to help the victims of some horrible misadventure. Newcomers to this form of TV writing need to watch the series, provide an idea and relate the facts. The studios will do the rest.

The second type of documentary is that which deals with subjects such as art, music, politics, war, morals, books or current affairs, which lend themselves to several programmes and in which various experts (including you) contribute their preferably exciting or controversial views. Examples of such programmes have included the *Gulf War* and *The Brains Trust* (a new version with a resident host). *Question Time* features four people of some note in their respective professions answering written questions from the audience and again there is a resident host.

In documentaries, whether single or series, the emphasis is to keep the audience glued to their seats. Even when there is an educational element in a programme (for example, a tour of London's museums; historic houses in the UK, the legacy of certain artists, musicians or kings), the programmes must be lively or riveting enough to prevent the switch being turned off.

The popularity of different TV programmes is constantly monitored not only by their producers, but by companies interested in getting the biggest audience for their advertised products. As an example, a media survey was made which related viewing behaviour to the ownership of financial products. One of the survey's results showed that in the year the survey was made, the top financial advertisers were Banks, Building Societies and Credit Cards. These companies took prime time when the most popular programmes were being shown.

But the biggest opportunity for the person who wants to write for TV today appears to be in talks or plays, or a series of dramatic episodes taking place in one place, town or neighbourhood. Such a 'fixed' setting helps keep costs down, as the same set can be used week after week. Hospitals are favourite venues; so are pubs and police stations, but not too closely recognisable areas.

How do you start your epic? As always, look at the market. Check what is being shown and what is finding favour with critics and public. The basic requirements of a TV play are theme plus story told by interesting characters speaking credible dialogue. Watch with a critical eye how it's done. Then, hopefully having learnt a few tips, chance your own arm.

Your scenes and sounds must grip your listeners immediately. There is no time wasting in TV. Action first, explanations later is the method here, sometimes to such an extent that the poor viewer is shown so many characters and scenes in the first couple of seconds that he or she can hardly follow the tale at all and switches off not because of too little action but too much.

What has been said in the chapter on radio plays applies to television drama also. The vital differences are that background, emotions and props are all visual, not aural. Sound, important though it is, serves to heighten the effects of the drama being enacted, not to create them.

The other big difference both from live theatre and radio plays is that TV goes in the early part of the evening at least to a (mainly) family audience with other attractions around. Each member of the audience may have different ideas of what to do/see. Your play must have the pulling power to stop any of them from turning or asking to turn on another channel.

Subjects of general human interest usually prove the most acceptable, though controversial themes (and scenes) are welcomed (perhaps too much so) for later 'slots'. The essence of a play is conflict, which is eventually resolved, or will be in the final episode. The conflicts can be of many kinds. Another ingredient, unless the work is an adaptation of some slow novel, or a series spread over many weeks, is speed.

As an example of how to submit your work, an important

TV (With Specimen Script)

part of selling it, here is the script of a very successful commercial by CDP Financial Partnership who produced it for Guardian Royal Exchange (now Guardian Assurance Company.)

CLIENT
PRODUCT
MEDIA   TV (60 secs)
TITLE

Vision	**Sound**
The commercial begins in a suburban street. We see a smart young insurance salesman at the gate of an ordinary suburban house. He opens the gate. A growl is heard. The salesman casually produces a dog biscuit from his pocket and throws it in the direction of the growl. He proceeds to the door and rings the bell. We hear a deadlock being freed. The door is partially opened. From within, we hear the voice of a woman.	**NATURAL SOUND EFFECTS**
	WOMAN: Yes?
	INS MAN: You remember I've come to talk to you about life insurance?
The salesman politely shows his ID card.	**WOMAN:** Oh yes, of course. Do come in.

30 Ways To Make Money – IN WRITING

We then see that the voice belongs to a pleasant woman in her early to mid thirties. She releases the chain and opens the door. The salesman appears slightly nonplussed.

We then cut inside to the sitting room.

A tray of tea is on a low table. On one side, the salesman sits on a sofa with his briefcase beside him. On the other side, the woman leans forward from her chair and pours tea.

The salesman looks around the room. the camera zooms in on something which has caught his attention, a family photograph on the mantlepiece.

INS MAN: Nice room, lovely family, but if you lost your husband – perish the thought – what would be left with?

The salesman rummages through his policies.

WOMAN: Freedom!

INS MAN: *(laughs politely)* Then perhaps you should consider. . .

TV (With Specimen Script)

The salesman rummages through his policies.	**WOMAN:** *(interrupting)* No need. . .
	INS MAN: Then what about a policy that would. . .
The salesman rummages through his policies.	
	WOMAN: *(interrupting)* Covered!
	INS MAN: Well here's a policy that could. . .
	WOMAN: *(interrupting)* No. . .
	INS MAN: *(flummoxed)* But?
The woman suddenly produces a Freedom brochure from beneath a cushion.	
	WOMAN: *(interrupting)* Maybe you don't know about Freedom?
Extra close up (ECU) at the salesman's stunned look as he surveys the brochure.	
	INS MAN: Freedom?
Camera back to woman.	
	WOMAN: The life insurance you can change as you go along. Look you're a young man, why go through life buying a new policy

30 Ways To Make Money – IN WRITING

	every time something happens? You know, when you get married, when you have kides, when you get a mortgaqge, when you invest,and should the worst happen, perish the thought...
The salesman hurriedly begins to gather his policies together. He gets up to leave and makes his exit as swiftly as he can. taking the Freedom brochure with him.	
	INS MAN: Well I mustn't take up any more of your time.
The camers stays on the woman, we hear noises of the dog barking at the salesman on the other side of the door.	**SOUND EFFECT:** dog growling
	WOMAN: (ite herself)... perhaps I should have mentioned there's hospital cover too.

The vision fades with a free phone number, the necessary financial warning that the "value of units can go down as well as up" and dissolves to the firm's logo.

Voice over (V/O) emphasises the message of the commercial with the words: "Freedom: the life insurance you can change as you go along". Then comes the name Guardian Assurance, and the fade out.

The series of advertisements for Allied Dunbar are further examples of successful commercials projecting financial products. They use the excellent jingle, 'There may be trouble ahead', with shots of ordinary people at certain kinds of crises in their lives.

Advertising of this kind is worth studying because, though so short, it emphasises for anybody aspiring to write for TV the two essential ingredients of the craft, namely how to attract and how to hold an audience's attention.

Appendix: Further Reading

BASIC
A dictionary, a book of quotations and an encyclopaedia for looking up facts, current events, centenaries and topical dates; an atlas and any similar aids to accuracy.

For help with grammar, spelling or vocabulary, any good text book or: *Getting to Grips with Writing* by C. Hilton and M. Hyder (Letts Educational '92) deals with "the rules and possibilities of written English, whether for business, study or general self improvement."

MORE ADVANCED
Editing and Design by Harold Evans, former editor of *The Sunday Times*. Book one of this five volume manual (I never saw the other four), *Newsman's English*, is a gold mine of information and inspiration on stringing words together for style, accuracy, impact. Chapter two contains five excellent rules.

Plain Words by Sir Ernest Gower offers wisdom and wit without Harold Evans' dynamism.

GUIDES (A) GENERAL
Guide for Authors (Basil Blackwell '85): 56 pages on what to look out for when assessing publishers, what to expect at different stages of publication and how to prepare a typescript.

Writing in Action by Paul Mills (Routledge '96): A guide to the process of writing with the emphasis on creative writing, it also covers autobiographical writing, reports and essays. "A book about process rather than product it also looks at adaptation and editing."

Writer's Questions Answered by Gordon Wells (Allison & Busby '91): Comprehensive answers to the questions most frequently asked at

155

writers' circles, conferences and weekend schools. Covers copyright, agents and royalties as well as the mechanics of writing.

How to Publish a Book by Robert Spicer (How to Books '95): A practical step-by-step guide to independent publishing.

GUIDES (B) STYLE:

The Oxford Writers' Dictionary : the essential style guide compiled by R. E. Allen tells you whether it's gipsy or gypsy; Razzmatazz or razzmatazz and so on.

Style Guide (The Economist) based on *The Economist's* own house style manual; invaluable for everyone who wants to communicate with clarity, style, precision.

On Newspaper Style by columnist Keith Waterhouse, versatile, brilliant and prolific author of plays and novels, writes with wit and sparkle a manual on the art of clear, correct and effective English.

ANTHOLOGIES

Any dictionary of quotations, for example,
Penguin Dictionary of Quotations by J. M. & M. J. Cohen.

Shakespearean Quotations in every day use: A Key to their Source and Context by L. L. Marsden.

A Shakespeare Glossary by C. T. Onions (Oxford) defines words and phrases used by Shakespeare.

A Shakespeare Companion by F. E. Halliday gives an invaluable précis of plots and people.

LITERARY INFORMATION

The Oxford book of Literary Anecdotes edited by James Sutherland: most readable tales about literary figures from Caedmon (circa AD 670) who could read but couldn't sing to proof readers who could read but couldn't proof, with excellent source material and index.

Appendix: Further Reading

The Oxford Companion to Literature: A comprehensive list of authors, books and characters edited by Margaret Drabble.

The Oxford Companion to Classical Literature: Sir Paul Harvey.

The Faber Book of Reportage edited by John Carey: eye witness accounts of great events, well written, vivid, immediate and firsthand.

FACT SOURCES
Any good encyclopaedia such as *Pears'*.
Chambers Dictionary of Dates: for anniversaries, including birthdays of the famous for every day of the year.

MARKETING
BRAD advertising media lists nearly 2,000 entries in alphabetical sections such as Business, Consumer, Electronic and Outdoor with their advertising rates.

Benn's Media Directory provides details of every journal published throughout the world with names of editors and advertising rates.

Writers' & Artists' Year Book and *The Writer's Handbook:* indispensable.

Sell Your Writing (Society of Authors) by Andrew Nash: highly readable 23 pages on marketing your work. Also from the Society: *Quick Guides on Buying a Word Processor, Publishing Contracts* and *Income Tax*.

SPECIALISED AND GENRE WRITING
This is the area in which, if you are going to make a million from your writing, you are most likely to make it.

Legal thrillers: following the success of *The Firm, The Client,* John Grisham's paperback *The Chamber* sold over a million copies and grossed over £6m.

Action thrillers: *Without Remorse* by Tom Clancy (sales 3.5m); *Decider* by Dick Francis (2.3m); Jeffrey Archer: *Eagle Trap* (0.5m).

Romance: Catherine Cookson: *The Golden Straw* (sales 2.9m), *The Year of the Virgins* (2.2m); Barbara T. Bradford: *Angel* (2.4m).

The aga saga: discreet romance in a mainly middle class domestic setting: Joanna Trollope: *The Rector's Wife; The Spanish Lover* (2.7m).

Crime: Patricia Cornwell: *Cruel and Unusual* (sales 2.1m) and the sleuths of Ruth Rendell, P. D. James.

Biographies and autobiographies: *Wild Swans*, by Jung Chang, sold over 5m but 'biogs' and 'autobiogs' are mostly written by people already famous such as politicians or sportspeople (Ian Botham made over £1m on his life story).

ADVICE ON SPECIAL AND GENRE WRITING:

Magazine Journalism Today by Anthony Davis (Heinemann).

The Way to Write for Television: Eric Paice (Elm Tree Books).

Writing a Play by Steve Gooch (A & C Black).

Handbook of Short Story Writing: Writers' Digest Books, Cincinnati, Ohio.

How To Write Stories for Magazines: Donna Baker (Allison & Busby): comprehensive, bright, enthusiastic.

How To Write the Story of Your Life: Frank P. Thomas (Writers' Digest).

How To Write & Sell Humour: Gene Perret (Writers' Digest).

To Writers with Love: lively, affectionate book on writing romantic novels by skilled practitioner, Mary Wibberley (Buchan & Enright).

How to Write a Damn Good Novel: A damn good title from American academic James N. Frey (Macmillan).

How to Write a Song: simple, practical guide by Rolf Harris.

Appendix: Further Reading

USEFUL ADDRESSES

Society of Authors 84 Drayton Gardens, London SW10 9SD

Arts Council of England 14 Great Peter Street, London, SW1 3NQ; of Northern Ireland 185 Stranmillis Road, Belfast BT9 5DU; of Wales 9 Museum Place, Cardiff CF1 3NX; Scottish Arts Council 12 Manor Place, Edinburgh EH3 7DD

Book Trust 45 East Hill, Wandsworth, London SW18 2QZ

British Film Institute 21 Stephen Street, London W1P 1PL

The Composers' Guild of Great Britain 34 Hanway Street, London W1P 9DE

British Kinematograph, Sound and Television Society M6–14, Victoria House, Vernon Place, London WC1B 4DF.

Mechanical Copyright Protection Society (MCPS) Elgar House, 41 Streatham High Road, London SW16 1ER

Music Publishers' Association (MPA) 3rd Floor, Strandgate, 18/20 York Buildings, London WC2N 6JU

National Union of Journalists Acorn House, 314 Gray's Inn Road, London WC1X 8DP

Performing Rights Society 29–33 Berners Street, London W1P 4AA

Screenwriters' Workshop 84 Wardour Street, London W1V 3LF

Theatre Writers' Union 1a Tower Street, London WC2H 9NP

For an up to date list of the full 30 Ways... series and our finance and investment books, please write to: The Rushmere Wynne Group PLC, 4-5 Harmill, Grovebury Road, Leighton Buzzard LU7 8FF.